REPRESENTATION AND PRESIDENTIAL PRIMARIES

REPRESENTATION AND PRESIDENTIAL PRIMARIES

The Democratic Party in the Post-Reform Era

JAMES I. LENGLE

CONTRIBUTIONS IN POLITICAL SCIENCE, NUMBER 57

Greenwood Press
Westport, Connecticut • London, England

810283

Library of Congress Cataloging in Publication Data

Lengle, James I 1949–
    Representation and Presidential primaries.

    (Contributions in political science; no. 57
ISSN 0147-1066)
    Bibliography: p.
    Includes index.
        1. Presidents—United States—Nomination.
2. Primaries—United States. 3. Representative
government and representation—United States.
4. Democratic Party. I. Title. II. Series.
JK522.L46   324.5′4′0973   80-1791
ISBN 0-313-22482-X (lib. bdg.)

Library of Congress Catalog Card Number: 80-1791
ISBN 0-313-22482-X
ISSN: 0147-1066

First published in 1981

Greenwood Press
A division of Congressional Information Service, Inc.
88 Post Road West, Westport, Connecticut 06881

Printed in the United States of America

10 9 8 7 6 5 4 3 2 1

To Pat, with love,
gratitude, and admiration

CONTENTS

TABLES

FIGURES

ACKNOWLEDGMENTS

MY THANKS run wide and deep. I would like to thank the State Data Program and the Survey Research Center at the University of California at Berkeley for supplying the Field data and for providing the technical assistance to process it. I would also like to thank the *New York Times*, *Time* Magazine, and Yankelovich, Skelly, and White, Inc., for their permission to use their 1972 primary election surveys. They of course bear no responsibility for the analyses and interpretations presented here. Gary Orren and William Schneider deserve special mention for graciously sharing that data.

I would like to thank Nelson Polsby and Raymond Wolfinger for their comments and suggestions on earlier drafts and for their friendship, support, and encouragement which proved just as invaluable.

I am deeply indebted to Byron Shafer, whose roles ranged from editor, to critic, to advisor, and whose contributions far outweigh mere words of thanks.

Finally, and most importantly, I dedicate this book to Pat who, more than anyone else, is responsible for its completion.

REPRESENTATION
AND PRESIDENTIAL
PRIMARIES

PRESIDENTIAL PRIMARIES AND REPRESENTATION: AN INTRODUCTION

HISTORICALLY, POLITICIANS, journalists, and political scientists alike have tended to dismiss the presidential primary as a showy but basically inconsequential part of American politics.[1] President Harry S. Truman, upon learning that his name had been entered in the 1952 New Hampshire primary without his consent, withdrew from the contest by announcing that primaries were mere "eyewash" and of no political consequence once the national convention actually met.[2]

Twenty-five years later, journalist Arthur T. Hadley took an impressionistic look at the intervening two hundred primaries and concluded by echoing Truman's sentiments. "Far from being decisive politically, the primaries appear more as a ritual encounter, a symbolic show whose results reinforce a victory already decided."[3] According to Hadley, the critical battles for the presidency are fought long before the first state primaries or the national convention are held. "Primarily in today's world, but also historically, the invisible primary [defined as the period of time between the election of one president and the holding of the first primary to determine the next] is where the winning candidate is actually selected."[4]

Social scientists, armed with mathematical measures, have not often seen cause to differ. Keech and Matthews, for instance, after examining the nomination process of the party in control of the presidency from 1936 to 1972 concluded that:

Viewed quantitatively, the impact of the presidential primaries on nominations within the party in power is not impressive. In eight of the last ten nominations the dominant position of the front runner before the primaries remained essentially unchanged at the end.... In all eight cases the candidate maintained the lead throughout the primary period and was ultimately nominated.[5]

The impact of presidential primaries on the nomination process within the out-party, a case where primaries might be expected to play a more prominent role, was also found negligible:

The record of the presidential primary system as it has operated in the opposition party since 1936 can thus be summed up as follows: When the party has a single front-runner, the primaries rarely change the situation. When the competitive situation within the party is more confused (1940, 1948, 1952, 1964), the primary system does little to facilitate the emergence of a single leader of the party.[6]

In sum, "primaries rarely have much independent effect on nomination outcomes."[7]

Some students of the history of American politics, however, view the role of presidential primaries differently.[8] In *Presidential Primaries: Road to the White House* political scientist James W. Davis offers Wendell Willkie, Harold Stassen, Dwight Eisenhower, John Kennedy, and Barry Goldwater as candidates whose fortunes were crucially shaped in primaries.[9] To this cast of contenders, he adds Harry S. Truman, who withdrew from the 1952 Democratic race after suffering a crushing defeat in that same New Hampshire primary which just days earlier he had dismissed as eyewash.

Theodore White, journalist and close observer of four presidential campaigns, also credits primaries with substantial, if not beneficial, influence:

In primaries, ambitions spurt from nowhere; unknown men carve their mark; old men are sent relentlessly to their political graves; bosses and leaders may be humiliated or unseated.... Primaries suck up and waste large sums of money from contributors who might better be tapped for the November finals; the charges and countercharges of primary civil war provide the enemy party with ammunition it can later use with blast effect against whichever primary contender emerges victorious; primary campaigns exhaust the candidate, use up his speech material, drain his vital energy, and leave him limp before he clashes with the major enemy.[10]

Putting primaries into a broader, more historical perspective, White concludes that they "were, and remain, vital to the play of American Presidential politics."[11]

Although the jury remains deadlocked over the historical import of primaries, a verdict can easily be reached about their more recent role. Primaries today have reached a level of importance unequaled in their seventy-year history and unmatched by any other formal component of the nomination process including the national convention itself. This increased importance is the result of two major developments: the increase both in the total number of primaries held and in the proportion of convention delegates chosen by primaries, and procedural changes in the way primaries are conducted (abolishing winner-take-all primaries, forcing delegate choice along predetermined guidelines, tightening the link between primary outcomes and delegate preferences).[12]

The number of states holding presidential primaries has increased dramatically. As table 1 shows, in 1968 only seventeen states held Democratic primaries and only sixteen states held Republican primaries. Between 1968 and 1972, six states switched from party caucuses and conventions to party primaries, raising the total number of Democratic and Republican primaries to twenty-three and twenty-two, respectively. By 1976, the number had jumped to twenty-nine for the Democrats and twenty-eight for the Republicans. Not since the early formative period of presidential primaries (from 1904 to 1916) has the nation witnessed such a sharp increase in the number of primaries, and never before has the total equaled that of 1976.

Of even more importance, has been the rise in the proportion of delegates chosen by primaries. Table 1 shows that in 1968 only 38 percent of all Democratic convention delegates and 34 percent of all Republican convention delegates were selected in primaries. By 1976 the proportion had increased to an overwhelming majority, 73 percent for the Democrats, 68 percent for the Republicans.

The resurgent and dominant position of presidential primaries in both parties' nomination processes is clearly evidenced in presidential nominations since 1968. Since that year only two of the six pre-primary front-runners have emerged with their party's nomination. Both victors were Republican incumbents, but neither escaped opposition—opposition lured into battle by the opportunities primaries presented. Richard M. Nixon was renominated in 1972 with only mild harassment from his party's right and left wings. But, even then, both opponents, Congressmen Paul N. "Pete" McCloskey and John Ashbrook, recognized that presidential primaries provided the only avenue for unseating an incumbent. Underfinanced and outmanned, they proceeded to chal-

Table 1
Proliferation of Presidential Primaries, 1968–1976

	DEMOCRATS			REPUBLICANS		
	1968	1972	1976	1968	1972	1976
Number of states	17	23	29	16	22	28
Number of delegates	983	1862	2183	458	710	1533
Percent of all delegates	38%	61%	73%	34%	53%	68%

SOURCE: Austin Ranney, *Participation in American Presidential Nominations, 1976* (Washington, D.C.: American Enterprise Institute, 1976), p. 6.

lenge the incumbent in primary after primary, hoping to crack his support within the party, to build momentum of their own, and eventually, to deny him the nomination. Neither succeeded.

In 1976 the incumbent president, Gerald R. Ford, faced a much stiffer test—twenty-eight primaries from which a majority of delegates to the Republican national convention would be selected—and a more formidable opponent, California's governor, Ronald Reagan. Here again, the opposition concentrated on the primaries. Unlike 1972, however, the challenger almost succeeded since Reagan fell just one hundred delegates short of stealing the nomination from a campaigning incumbent—a feat never before accomplished in the 150 year history of national conventions, but now made possible by the proliferation of primaries.

In the remaining four campaigns, someone other than the front-runner did capture the nomination, and primaries did play a decisive role in determining who the nominee would and would not be. In 1968 Lyndon Johnson, a sitting Democratic president eligible for renomination, withdrew from the race after a media-declared loss to Eugene McCarthy in the New Hampshire Democratic primary. Johnson's withdrawal prompted New York's senator, Robert F. Kennedy, to enter. Kennedy's subsequent primary victories, in turn, were enough to deny the nomination to McCarthy.

Republican front-runners were not immune to the fatal sting of primaries either. In the Republican campaign of 1968, Governor George Romney of Michigan was at the top of the all-important Gallup poll standings. His misguided statement about Vietnam "brainwashing" and early polls that showed him losing to Richard Nixon by a six-to-one margin in the New Hampshire Republican primary prompted his withdrawal. Richard Nixon, the winner in New Hampshire that year, eventually emerged as the GOP standard-bearer after outdueling all other contenders in the remaining primaries.

In the 1972 Democratic race, Maine's senator, Edmund S. Muskie, was the odds-on favorite to win the nomination. But Senator George S. McGovern, languishing at 2 percent in the early Gallup polls, captured the nation's attention with a strong showing in New Hampshire, and then went on to win the Democratic nomination after emerging victorious in Wisconsin and California. In 1976 Governor Jimmy Carter of Georgia, whose initial Gallup poll ranking matched George McGovern's for anonymity, received the Democratic nod after coming out ahead in a field of ten challengers in the early primaries. As recent political history readily attests, presidential primaries *can* unseat incumbent presidents, *can* untrack party front-runners, and *can* transform aspiring political unknowns into major party nominees. Presidential primaries have become, without a doubt, the only "Road to the White House."

The glamor and drama of presidential primaries did not escape the notice of the national news media. Because of the decisive impact of primaries, some networks considered eliminating their gavel-to-gavel coverage of presidential nominating conventions. Herbert S. Schlosser, former president of NBC, stated:

If there is a real contest at the convention, full coverage may be indicated. If, however, the convention is merely an initiation rite for a candidate who has locked up the nomination in the primaries, the extent of our coverage will be determined accordingly.[13]

Unfortunately, despite their widely recognized stature, presidential primaries have received little scholarly attention. Most of the existing research focuses on the state and local level.[14] The few works which deal specifically with presidential primaries are limited by being either historically descriptive accounts of players and outcomes,[15] or large-scale analyses of voter turnout.[16] Consequently, an examination of electoral behavior in presidential primaries, focused on the question of voter representation, and in light of the Democratic party's role as an instrument for aggregating and translating public wishes into public policy, may prove useful.

The method both parties use to select their presidential nominee has changed considerably over the past 200 years.[17] The nomination process employed by the Democratic and Republican parties today would be unrecognizable to Democrats and Federalists of the early nineteenth century, to Democrats and Republicans of the late nineteenth century, and even, perhaps, to Democrats and Republicans in the early twentieth century. Many of the changes, whether the result of natural political evolution or deliberate political reform, have had the appearance of democratizing the selection process by increasing the number, and presumably, the representativeness of the participants. Figure 1 depicts the historical development of the presidential nomination process and traces the gradual incorporation of the party hierarchy and rank and file into the party's most important decision-making process.

For the first one hundred years, reform of the presidential nominating process revolved around the question of who among the party elite should control the decision-making process. As figure 1 shows, each level of the party hierarchy had its turn. Initially, the presidential nominee was selected by the party's nationally elected officeholders via a national legislative caucus. Later, the party's state officeholders chose the nominee in state legislative caucuses. Finally, at the close of the nineteenth century, the party's state and local officials took control through state and local conventions and caucuses. Reformers viewed each change as an improvement over its predecessor since each step further decentralized control and incorporated more of the party struc-

FIGURE 1   Development of the Presidential Nomination Process

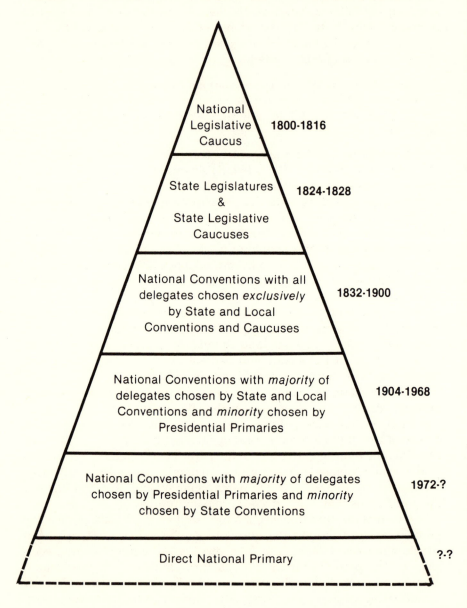

ture into the nomination process. But, in time, each change spawned its own set of problems and critics and eventually became the target of a new round of reform.

It was not until the twentieth century and the advent of presidential primaries that the delegate-selection process was formally opened to the party rank and file. Primaries, like their predecessors, were also viewed as instruments for furthering democracy in what were considered to be boss-ruled and oligarchically controlled parties. In the opinion of their advocates, primaries democratized the nomination process by transferring the responsibility for delegate selection from the party professionals to the party rank and file. Party members replaced the party elite as decision makers; elections replaced caucuses and conventions as decision-making forums. Such a process, it was argued, was more in keeping with the basic democratic precepts upon which the country was founded.

Besides conforming to traditional democratic norms, primaries were also viewed by their advocates as saviors of the party system itself. In the short run, their argument goes, primaries help parties achieve their immediate goal of winning elections because the most popular candidate among the contenders becomes the nominee. In the long run, both major parties become stronger due to the active participation of their adherents; they become more responsive because prospective nominees must appeal directly to the needs and interests of the party membership; and they become more competitive since both parties will be represented in the general election by their strongest candidate.

Needless to say, theory and practice are not necessarily so closely linked. Conditions and assumptions present during the deductive stage of theorizing are often absent from real world events. Unfortunately, in time, most arguments become regenerative, regardless of the empirical validity of the assumptions and conditions on which they were based. Initial assumptions are either forgotten or accepted as part of reality without much serious testing.

So it is with presidential primaries. The benefits to the party system, and to democracy, that the proponents of primaries carefully deduced were premised upon one of two conditions: the participation of all party members or the participation of a representative cross section of the party rank and file. If neither of these conditions is met, the effect of primaries on the party system becomes unpredictable—and perhaps even perverse.

In the short run, a minute and unrepresentative primary electorate gives disproportionate power to specific, limited groups. This may affect the types of issues stressed, the types of candidates chosen, and hence, the party's chances for success in the general election. In the medium run, the effect may be to mold party candidates more and more toward the image, style, and issue-orientation of that sector of the party stimulated by circumstances to participate in primaries.[18] By the same token, party candidates may become less and less ready to take into account those elements of the party indisposed by circumstances to play a role in the primary. Ultimately, of course, due to the perpetual and subtle conditioning of elites, masses, and issues, the structure and operation of both political parties may be substantially and permanently altered.

In testing how well reality conforms with theory, it takes little in the way of empirical research to reject the first condition of universal participation. The mean turnout for the seventy-two presidential primaries held from 1948 to 1968 in which voters had the opportunity to vote directly (in presidential preference polls) or indirectly (in choosing among slates of delegates pledged to particular aspirants) for their presidential preference was only 27 percent.[19] Of these seventy-two primaries, only one (Oregon, 1968) had a turnout exceeding 50 percent. In many of these cases, of course, there was no serious contest in one or both parties' primaries, and in others the contestants did not include a major national contender. But even after controlling for competitiveness, the average turnout in contested states climbs to only 39 percent.[20]

In 1976 the record was even more discouraging. The twenty-six states for which turnout can be computed (using voting age population) had a mean turnout of only 28 percent.[21] This ranged from a low of 12 percent in New Jersey and Rhode Island, to a high of only 44 percent in Oregon.[22] The twenty-two states classified as competitive in 1976 had a mean turnout of only 28 percent—a drop of eleven percentage points from the figure for the 1948–1968 period.[23] If indications point to a more important role for primaries, but to a declining rather than increasing participatory role for the American population in those primaries, then the case for primaries rests solely on assumptions of representativeness.

The first political scientist to predict the risk of unrepresentative primary electorates was V. O. Key. Almost twenty years ago, he wrote:

The effective primary constituency . . . may come to consist predominantly of the people of certain sections of a state, of persons of specified national origin or religious affiliation, of people especially responsive to certain styles of political leadership or shades of ideology, or of other groups markedly unrepresentative in one way or another of the party following.[24]

To date, few political scientists have considered this warning at the presidential primary level, and only Austin Ranney has put it under rigorous empirical study.[25] By comparing voters with nonvoters in the 1968 Wisconsin presidential primary, and by comparing intenders with nonintenders in the 1968 New Hampshire primary, Ranney discovered that those who voted (or intended to vote) were in several respects quite unrepresentative of those who did not. Voters were older, richer, more active in civic, religious, and political organizations, and more likely to hold stronger opinions about the issues of the day.

Ranney's findings have been tested in an examination of the 1972 and 1968 California Democratic presidential primaries using Mervin Field's polls of California's voting-age population.[26] The data used have three clear advantages not found in Ranney's. First, the data were collected by a single organization asking identical questions of similarly derived samples over time.[27] Thus, the presence, direction, and magnitude of demographic representativeness can be empirically tested in two different campaigns involving two different sets of candidates and issues. Second, the data were collected in a state that, unlike New Hampshire and Wisconsin, possesses a demographic and ideological diversity more characteristic both of the Democratic party in most large, urban, industrialized states, and indeed, of the Democratic party nationwide. Third, in both California primaries the major contenders were on the ballot; the campaigns were consequently hotly contested and highly competitive, and were, as a result, significant in crowning one presidential nominee (McGovern, 1972) and retiring another (McCarthy, 1968). Given these data and a set of optimal political circumstances, the California primaries are nearly ideal for studying the representative quality of Democratic presidential primaries.

A second major difference between Ranney's research and this study is the application of the concept of representation. Ranney tests for the electorate's representativeness by comparing voters in Wisconsin and intenders in New Hampshire with nonvoters in Wisconsin and nonintenders in New Hampshire. In defense of this approach he states:

I have chosen the straight participant/nonparticipant comparison because I believe it more accurately operationalizes the concept of representation held by most party leaders who regard the primaries as the nominating systems most representative element. From what they say and do . . . it seems clear that most leaders assume a sharp distinction between the "representatives" (the convention delegates, the primary voters) and the "represented" (the party's grass roots supporters). If, as I believe, this concept of representation permeates most current political disputes about the proper organizational role of primaries and conventions, then accepting it rather than substituting a concept which regards the representatives as part of the represented seems likely to make our empirical findings more relevant to those disputes.[28]

A different, more conventional definition of representation is used in the following pages. The important empirical question, as originally posed by Key, is whether the primary electorate consists of groups markedly unrepresentative of the party following. The answer is found, not by comparing two mutually exclusive parts, that is, primary voters with nonvoters, but by comparing the part with the whole, that is, the primary electorate (voters) with the entire party membership. This view of representation currently dominates most political and social thinking and it is by this view that most political and social processes are currently being judged.[29]

NOTES

1. William R. Keech and Donald R. Matthews, *The Party's Choice* (Washington, D.C.: Brookings Institution, 1976); Arthur T. Hadley, *The Invisible Primary* (Englewood Cliffs, N.J.: Prentice-Hall, 1976); James R. Beniger, "Winning the Presidential Nomination: National Polls and State Primary Elections, 1936–1972" *Public Opinion Quarterly* 40 (Spring 1976): 22–38; William H. Lucy, "Polls, Primaries, and Presidential Nominations," *Journal of Politics* 35 (November 1973): pp. 830–48.

2. Paul T. David, Malcolm Moos, and Ralph M. Goldman, *Presidential Nominating Politics in 1952: The National Story* (Baltimore: Johns Hopkins Press, 1954), p. 37.

3. Hadley, *Invisible Primary*, p. 2.

4. Ibid., p. 1.

5. Keech and Matthews, *Party's Choice*, p. 96.

6. Ibid., p. 114.

7. Ibid., p. 229.

8. Nelson W. Polsby and Aaron Wildavsky, *Presidential Elections*, 4th ed. (New York: Charles Scribner's Sons, 1976); James David Barber, ed., *Choosing the President* (Englewood Cliffs, N.J.: Prentice-Hall, 1974); James Davis, *Presidential Primaries: Road to the White House* (New York: Crowell, 1967); Harry W. Ernst, *The Primary That Made A President: West Virginia, 1960* (New York: McGraw-Hill, 1962); Theodore White, *The Making of the President, 1960* (New York: Atheneum, 1961); Theodore White, *The Making of the President, 1964* (New York: Atheneum, 1965); Theodore White, *The Making of the President, 1968* (New York: Atheneum, 1969); Theodore White, *The Making of the President, 1972* (New York: Atheneum, 1973); Gerald M. Pomper, *Nominating the President* (New York: W. W. Norton, 1966).

9. Davis, *Presidential Primaries*, pp. 42–195.

10. White, *Making of the President, 1960*, pp. 85–86.

11. Ibid., p. 86.

12. For changes in Democratic party rules, *see* Commission on Party Structure and Delegate Selection, *Mandate for Reform* (Washington, D.C.: Democratic National Committee, 1970); Commission on Presidential Nomination and Party Structure, *Openness, Participation, and Party Building: Reforms for a Stronger Democratic Party* (Washington, D.C.: Democratic National Committee, 1979). For changes in Republican party rules, *see* The Delegates and Organization Commit-

tee, *Programming for the Party Future, Part 1* (Washington, D.C.: Republican National Committee, 1971); and *The Delegate Selection Procedures for the Republican Party, Part 2* (Washington, D.C.: Republican National Committee, 1971).

For an analysis of the effects of abolishing winner-take-all primaries, *see* James I. Lengle and Byron Shafer, "Primary Rules, Political Power, and Social Change," *American Political Science Review* 70 (March 1976): pp. 25–40.

For an analysis of the effects of the quota guidelines, *see* William Cavala, "Changing the Rules Changes the Game: Party Reform and the 1972 California Delegation to the Democratic National Convention," *American Political Science Review* 68 (March 1974): pp. 27–42.

13. *San Francisco Chronicle,* 16 October 1976.

14. Austin Ranney, "The Representativeness of Primary Electorates," *Midwest Journal of Political Science* 12 (May 1968): pp. 224–38; Austin Ranney and Leon D. Epstein, "The Two Electorates: Voters and Non-Voters in a Wisconsin Primary," *Journal of Politics* 28 (August 1966): pp. 598–616; V. O. Key, *American State Politics* (New York: Alfred A. Knopf, 1956), pp. 85–197.

15. Davis, *Presidential Primaries;* White, *Making of the President, 1960;* White, *Making of the President 1964;* White, *Making of the President, 1968;* White, *Making of the President, 1972;* Louise Overacker, *Presidential Primaries* (New York: Macmillan, 1926); Paul T. David, Malcolm Moos, and Ralph M. Goldman, eds., *Presidential Nominating Politics in 1952,* 5 vols. (Baltimore: Johns Hopkins Press, 1954).

16. Austin Ranney, "Turnout and Representation in Presidential Primary Elections," *American Political Science Review* 66 (March 1972): pp. 21–37; Austin Ranney, *Participation in American Presidential Nominations, 1976* (Washington, D.C.: American Enterprise Institute, 1977); William D. Morris and Otto Davis, "The Sport of Kings: Turnout in Presidential Preference Primaries" (Paper delivered at the 1975 American Political Science Association Convention, San Francisco, September, 1975.)

17. For an excellent account of these historical changes and the motivations behind them, *see* Austin Ranney, *Curing the Mischiefs of Factions: Party Reform in America* (Berkeley: University of California Press, 1975).

18. This point is made by V. O. Key in reference to state primaries in *American State Politics,* p. 153.

19. Ranney, "Turnout and Representation," p. 23.

20. Ibid., p. 24.

21. Ranney, *Presidential Nominations,* p. 21.

22. Ibid., p. 20.

23. Ibid., p. 22.

24. Key, *American State Politics,* p. 153.

25. Austin Ranney, "Turnout and Representation." *See also* Nelson Polsby, *Political Promises: Essays and Commentary in American Politics* (New York: Oxford University Press, 1974), pp. 31–34.

26. The California Poll data, originally collected by the Field Research Corporation, were provided by the State Data Program of the Institute of Governmental Studies, with the assistance of the Survey Research Center, University of California, Berkeley. Neither the original collectors of the data nor the Survey Research

Center bear any responsibility for the analyses and interpretations presented here.

27. Ranney's data for New Hampshire were taken from a pre-election survey of registered voters. His data for Wisconsin were taken from a post-election survey of the voting age population. In addition, the surveys were conducted by different research organizations. Recognizing the difficulties inherent in his data, Ranney himself states, "When considering the findings... one should bear in mind... differences in the New Hampshire and Wisconsin studies." Ranney, "Turnout and Representation," p. 25.

28. Ibid.

29. This view of representation is identical to the one Hanna Pitkin calls "descriptive representation." According to this view, a representative body is distinguished by an accurate correspondence or resemblance to what it represents. *See* Hanna Fenichel Pitkin, *The Concept of Representation* (Berkeley: University of California Press, 1967), pp. 60–91. Another useful book on the concept of representation is J. Roland Pennock and John W. Chapman, eds., *Representation: Nomos X* (New York: Atherton Press, 1968).

2

DEMOGRAPHIC REPRESENTATION IN PRESIDENTIAL PRIMARIES

> *The effective primary constituency . . . may come to consist predominantly of . . . groups markedly unrepresentative . . . of the party following.*
>
> V. O. Key

MEASURING THE presence, direction, and magnitude of demographic unrepresentativeness is a simple procedure. First, the terms "party membership" and "primary electorate" need to be defined. As used here, "party membership" (or rank and file) is defined as all Democratic party identifiers, and "primary electorate" is defined as all Democratic primary voters.[1]

The second step is to compare the percentages of the primary electorate and party membership that social or economic groups contribute. The best way to compare these distributions is to compute ratios between the percentage of the Democratic primary electorate that a given demographic group composes and its percentage of the party membership. These ratios reveal both the direction and magnitude of over-representation or under-representation for each socioeconomic group. For example, Democrats with an annual income of $20,000 or more composed 10 percent of the California Democratic party membership in 1972. If they formed only 5 percent of the primary electorate, they would be under-represented by 50 percent and therefore receive a Representation Ratio of −50. If, on the other hand, they formed 15 percent of the primary electorate, they would be over-represented by 50 percent, and therefore receive a score of +50.

This measure of over- and under-representation is identical to the one employed by Verba and Nie in *Participation in America* and similar to the one employed by Robert Dahl in *A Preface to Democratic Theory*.[2] The formal definition of the measure for any given demographic group is:

$$RR = \frac{Y_i - X_i}{X_i} \times 100$$

where: RR = Ratio of over- and under-representation
           X_i = The percentage of the Democratic party membership that a demographic group composes
           Y_i = The percentage of the Democratic primary electorate that a demographic group composes.

Table 2 presents Representation Ratios for various socioeconomic groups within the party. Positive signs indicate over-representation; negative signs, under-representation. The magnitude of over- and under-representation per group is reflected by the ratio itself.[3]

An examination of educational representation in 1972 quickly dispels any notions of demographically representative primary electorates. As groups, Democrats with an eighth-grade education or less, a ninth-to-eleventh grade education, and a high school education were under-represented in their party's primary electorate. Their respective scores of −10, −31, and −10 indicate that their percentage of the Democratic primary electorate was not commensurate with their percentage of the party membership but was 10 percent, 31 percent, and 10 percent smaller. Combined, these three groups formed 54 percent of all Democratic party identifiers, but they formed only 46 percent of the Democratic primary voters. This represents a switch for them from majority to minority status, courtesy of the California primary.

Conversely, over-representation increased with education. Democrats with one to three years of college education or business or technical training, were slightly over-represented (+4); Democrats with a college degree were even more over-represented (+33); while Democrats with an advanced college degree were the most over-represented contingent (+50).

The 1968 primary was skewed in the same direction. Although the magnitudes were smaller, less-educated Democrats (a high school degree or less) were again uniformly under-represented, while their better-educated counterparts (one year of college or more) were again uniformly over-represented.

An analysis of income presents a similar picture. In 1972 Democrats earning less than $3,000 were the most under-represented group (−18), although Democrats earning $3,000–$6,999 and $7,000–$9,999 followed closely behind (−11, −11). On the other hand, all income groups above $10,000 were over-represented, with the greatest disproportion occurring among Democrats earning over $20,000 (+30).

The 1968 primary followed the same pattern. Democrats earning under $3,000, or $3,000–$6,999 were under-represented; Democrats earning $10,000–$14,999, or over $15,000, were over-represented.

The category, occupation, offers similar findings.[4] In 1972 Democrats with blue-collar occupations (laborers, service workers, semiskilled

Table 2
Demographic Representation in Presidential Primaries

1972 CALIFORNIA PRIMARY		1968 CALIFORNIA PRIMARY	
Education		*Education*	
8th grade and under	−10	8th grade and under	−7
9th–11th grade	−31	9th–11th grade	−11
High school	−10	High school	−6
1–3 years college	+4	1–2 years college	+17
College degree	+33	3–4 years college[a]	+10
Advanced col. deg.	+50	Advanced col. deg.	+20
Income		*Income*	
Under $3,000	−18	Under $3,000	−25
$3,000–$6,999	−11	$3,000–$6,999	−11
$7,000–$9,999	−11	$7,000–$9,999	0
$10,000–$14,999	+3	$10,000–$14,999	+17
$15,000–$19,999	+17	Over $15,000[b]	+18
Over $20,000	+30		
Social Class		*Social Class*	
Lower class	−25	Lower class	−29
Lower middle class	−15	Lower middle class	−10
Middle class	+2	Middle class	+5
Upper mid/upper class	+20	Upper mid/upper class	+8
Occupation		*Occupation*	
Laborer/service	−11	Laborer/service	−14
Operative/semiskilled	−25	Operative/semiskilled	−8
Craft/skilled/foremen	−16	Craft/skilled/foremen	+17
Clerical/sales	+13	Clerical/sales	0
Prof/officials/mgrs	+10	Prof/officials/mgrs	+9
Race		*Race*	
White	+5	White	+1
Black	−17	Black	0
Asian/Spanish	−24	Asian/Spanish	−20

SOURCE: California Polls, 6804 and 7204, Field Research Corporation, San Francisco, Calif.
A score of "0" means perfect representation.
[a] No separate college degree category used in 1968.
[b] Highest income category used in 1968.

workers, craftsmen, foremen, skilled workers) were under-represented, while white-collar Democrats (sales personnel, clerical workers, officials, managers, semiprofessionals, professionals) were over-represented. In 1968 the same general pattern emerged, although the categories shifted slightly.

Because social class was measured partly as a function of education, income, and occupation, the ratios for these categories also fall in line with the previous findings.[5] In both 1968 and 1972 lower-class and lower middle-class Democrats were under-represented; middle-class and upper middle-class/upper-class Democrats were over-represented.

A comparison of racial distributions between the primary electorate and party membership reveals an under-representation of racial minorities and a corresponding over-representation of white Democrats for both years.

The parallel between 1968 and 1972 becomes even more striking when both years are compared on a group-by-group basis. In 1968 ten groups of Democrats, all lower socioeconomic status (SES) were under-represented. In 1972 the same ten groups of Democrats were again under-represented. In 1968 ten groups of Democrats, all upper SES, were over-represented; in 1972 nine of the same ten groups were again over-represented. As measured by the presence, direction, and magnitude of demographic unrepresentativeness in these California primaries, political history, despite a different cast of characters, issues, and stimuli, *does* repeat itself.

Given our knowledge of turnout and of the nature of party support in the United States, the above findings are not totally unexpected. Since their inception, all voting-behavior studies have shown turnout to vary by socioeconomic group.[6] Better-educated, higher-income, upper middle-class and upper-class individuals vote in greater proportions than their lower SES counterparts. For example, individuals with a college degree outvoted individuals with a grade school education by 21 percent in the 1964 presidential election, by 24 percent in the 1968 presidential election, and by 29 percent in the 1972 presidential election.[7]

The explanation for these differences is by now common wisdom. The greater an individual's education, the greater his political knowledge, his interest in the campaign, his sense of civic duty, and his feelings of political efficacy. These, in turn, form the motivational complex behind voter participation.[8] Since primaries are elections, and since all acts of voting require a certain degree of interest, motivation, and physical exertion, there is every reason to suspect that generalizations about turnout in general elections are just as applicable—and probably even more so—in primaries.

Variation in turnout is a necessary but not sufficient condition to produce unrepresentative primary electorates. Primaries do differ from general elections in one important respect—participation is usually restricted to party members. Therefore, it is also necessary that socioeconomic status be weakly or only moderately related to party membership. For example, even with variations in turnout, a class-based party system would be little affected by unrepresentative primary electorates.

To illustrate: suppose two or three parties existed in the United States, each with an exclusive base of support within one class, and closed primaries were conducted to choose the parties' nominees. Turnout would, of course, still vary by party. The lowest turnout would be recorded in the party of the lower class; the highest turnout, in the party of the upper class. But since party support would be relatively homogeneous, turnout would not vary significantly within each party. Hence, demographic unrepresentativeness and its attending consequences would not surface.

One need not resort to theoretical party systems as examples. Party support in many Western European democracies, especially in multiparty systems, is class-based.[9] In Britain, for instance, there is strong evidence that party allegiance follows class lines more strongly than anywhere else in the English-speaking world.[10] Finnish party politics are similarly aligned: 85 percent of the Finns who prefer the Agrarian party are farmers, and 82 percent of those supporting the Socialist parties are workers.[11] The modified three-party system in West German politics also runs along class lines.[12]

American parties, however, do not fit the European mold. Democratic party membership tends predominantly, but not exclusively, toward the lower end of the class scale. Republican party membership tends predominantly, but not exclusively, toward the upper end of the class scale. As one student of parties states, "Each of the major parties tends to have a somewhat different clientele of supporters among the groups in society. . . . Neither party has exclusive 'control' of any of the population groups. Each party is sufficiently heterogeneous to receive some support from all groups."[13] It is this unique blend of classless parties and class-related turnout that produces the particular direction and magnitude of unrepresentativeness found in Democratic primary electorates. A short analysis of these two conditions as they existed in 1972 and 1968 is presented below.

CALIFORNIA DEMOCRATIC PARTY IDENTIFICATION

Figure 2 presents California Democratic party identification by education, income, occupation, social class, and race. Surprisingly, in view of the popular notion of California as the home of a new, different, or deviant culture, California Democrats resemble their national counterparts to a remarkable degree.[14]

As figure 2-1 and 2-6 show, education and Democratic party affiliation are negatively related. In both years, Californians with an eighth grade education or less, a ninth- to eleventh-grade education, and a high school education were proportionally more Democratic than the state as

FIGURE 2 Democratic Party Identification by Socioeconomic Characteristics

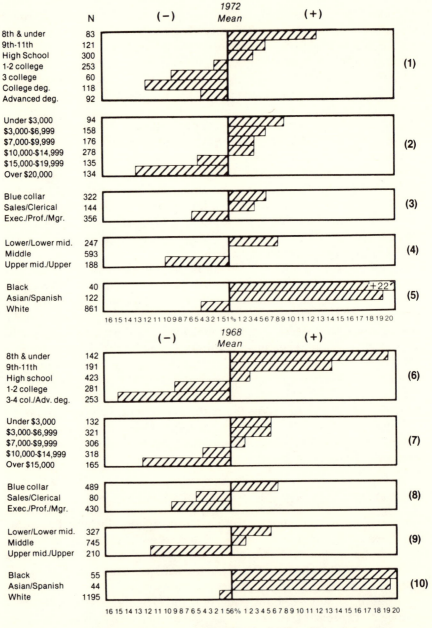

Source: California Polls 6804 and 7204, Field Research Corporation, San Francisco, Calif.

a whole. The highest percentage of Democratic affiliation was among Californians with the least amount of formal education. Conversely, better-educated individuals were proportionally less Democratic with the least support for the party coming from college-educated Californians. The gap between the two extremes is especially impressive. College-educated Californians were 24 percent less Democratic in 1972 and 34 percent less Democratic in 1968 than Californians with an eighth-grade education or less.

The remaining bar graphs in figure 2 also show negative relationships between Democratic party identification and socioeconomic characteristics. Disproportionate support in both years came from income groups below $10,000, blue collar workers, and the lower class/lower middle class. Racial minorities (blacks, Asians, Hispanics) were also overwhelmingly Democratic.

For the moment, the direction and strength of these relationships are unimportant. More central to an understanding of the source of demographic unrepresentativeness is the finding that support, nonetheless, does cross all socioeconomic categories. In 1972, Californians with a college degree were 24 percent less Democratic than Californians with an eighth-grade education. Nevertheless, two out of every five college-educated Californians thought of themselves as Democrats. Or, to take another example, Californians earning over $20,000 were 21 percent less Democratic than Californians earning under $3,000. Yet 38 percent of these wealthiest Californians were Democrats. Although figure 2 shows Democratic party identification concentrated toward the lower end of each socioeconomic category, it is not concentrated there exclusively. And it is this crosscutting support that sets the stage for unrepresentative primary electorates.

TURNOUT IN CALIFORNIA'S DEMOCRATIC PRESIDENTIAL PRIMARIES

The immediate explanation for recurring demographic unrepresentativeness is variation in turnout. If turnout were proportionally equal among Democrats at all socioeconomic levels (for example, 100 percent, 50 percent, or only 1 percent), then primary electorates would be an exact demographic replica of the party's rank and file. But turnout in general elections is socioeconomically related, not uniform, and there is no reason to suspect that turnout in primaries will be less so. Figure 3 presents 1972 and 1968 Democratic primary turnout by education, income, occupation, social class, and race.

Despite high turnouts in 1972 (66 percent) and 1968 (64 percent)—and high turnouts presumably repress this relationship—a relatively strong

FIGURE 3 Democratic Primary Turnout by Socioeconomic Characteristics

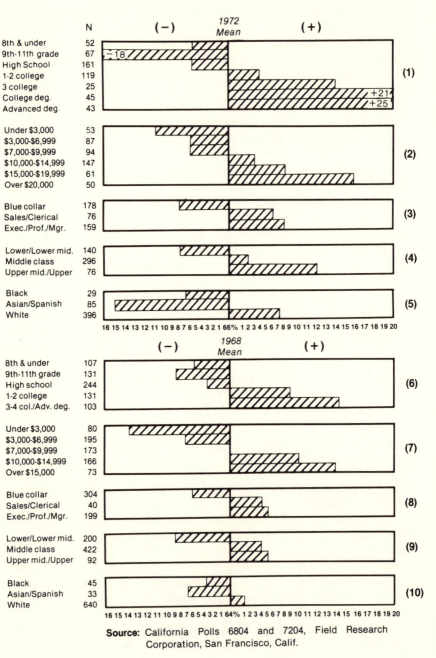

Source: California Polls 6804 and 7204, Field Research Corporation, San Francisco, Calif.

relationship existed between education and turnout. As Figure 3-1 shows, turnout in 1972 among Democrats with an eighth-grade education or less, Democrats with a ninth- to eleventh-grade education, and Democrats with a high school degree ranged from 18 percent to 6 percent below the state mean. In the same year, turnout among better educated Democrats ranged from 4 percent to 25 percent above the state average. Although the strength of the relationship is a bit weaker in 1968, Figure 3-6 shows that the direction remains the same.

Comparing differences between educational groups, rather than their differences from the mean, illustrates these variations even more clearly. For example, 91 percent of all Democrats with an advanced college degree cast ballots in 1972, but only 53 percent of all Democrats with a high school education or less did so—a difference of 38 percent. The turnout for these two groups in 1968 was 78 percent and 57 percent, respectively. Needless to say, these substantial variations produced the particular direction and magnitude of educational unrepresentativeness discovered in both primary electorates.

The direction and strength of the relationship between turnout and income for both years were also remarkably similar. Figure 3-2 and 3-7 show that turnout increased with income in both years. In 1972 (figure 3-2) turnout among Democrats with incomes below $10,000 fell short of the state average, with the lowest turnout registered by Democrats with incomes under $3,000 (55 percent, or 11 percent below the state mean). In contrast, all income groups above $10,000 exceeded the state mean, with the highest turnout found among Democrats with earnings in excess of $20,000 (82 percent, or 16 percent above the state mean). The difference between the lowest (under $3,000) and highest income categories (over $20,000) was 27 percent.

The figures for 1968 (figure 3-7) were almost identical. Compared to a statewide turnout of 64 percent, only 50 percent of all Democrats earning under $3,000 and 57 percent of all Democrats earning between $3,000–$6,999, cast ballots for their favorite presidential contenders. In contrast, Democrats earning $10,000–$14,999 and over $15,000 surpassed the state average by 10 percent and 14 percent, respectively, and outvoted their low income counterparts by 24 percent and 28 percent.

Examining Democratic turnout in 1972 and 1968 by occupation, social class, and race also reveals substantial variations. White-collar Democrats outvoted blue-collar Democrats by 16 percent in 1972 and by 12 percent in 1968; upper-middle-class and upper-class Democrats outvoted lower middle-class and lower-class Democrats by 20 percent in 1972 and by 14 percent in 1968; white Democrats outvoted Democrats from racial minorities by 18 percent in 1972 and by 6 percent in 1968. Consequently, equal representation of occupations, social classes, and race, like education and income, was far from realized in both years. Without a doubt, the picture of primary electorates slowly emerging from the California experience tends to confirm V. O. Key's twenty-year-old untested suspicions.

PARTISANSHIP AND REPRESENTATION

In one sense, the ideal situation for any political party that relies upon rank-and-file control of the nomination process is 100 percent turnout. This guarantees representation of all party members and selection of the candidate who can garner the broadest first-choice support among all Democrats.

Given the reality of limited participation and the absence of a workable prescription for attaining the textbook ideal, presidential primaries could still be saved from unrepresentativeness by proportionally equal turnout. Under this condition, representation would be at least commensurate with strength inside the party. But, as shown in the preceeding section, turnout in primaries is strongly related to socioeconomic characteristics of Democrats.

Although political theorists might be repelled by anything less than perfect demographic representation (resulting from either universal or proportionally equal turnout), practicing politicians might readily accept, and even warmly embrace, unrepresentativeness if it were strongly related to partisanship; that is, if overrepresentation occurred among socioeconomic groups disproportionately Democratic in party identification. The symbiotic relationship that exists between a party and its adherents would then be reinforced since groups from whom the party receives disproportionate support, and to whom party policy is directed, would be exercising disproportionate influence in the nomination process. The end result might even be a stronger, more responsive party for which unrepresentative primary electorates could take credit.

This line of reasoning, of course, would not apply equally to majority and minority parties in a two party system. A majority party, like the Democratic party, can win presidential elections without having to attract minority party support. Thus, for them, a nomination process which gives disproportionate influence to traditional party identifiers is more likely to produce a candidate with the strong intraparty appeal that is needed for electoral victory in November. A minority party, on the other hand, needs majority party defections. Thus, a similar situation in the Republican primaries might prove disastrous in November.

In order to determine if traditional Democratic party identifiers are advantaged by unrepresentativeness, or, as Key wondered, whether the "primary constituency... may come to consist... of groups... unrepresentative... of the party following," the partisanship of socio-economic groups is compared in table 3 with their degree of representation in primaries. All socioeconomic groups with Democratic party identification above the state average (*see* figure 2) are listed as "D" in table 3. All groups with Democratic party identification below the state average are listed as "R." All groups with positive representation ratios (that is, over-represented in the primary) are listed as "+." All groups with negative representation ratios (that is, under-represented in the primary) are listed as " −." If the redeeming quality of unrepresenta-tiveness exists, then the most Democratically partisan groups should also be the most over-represented groups. The findings in table 3 should be disconcerting to (democratic) theorists and (Democratic) politicians alike. Table 3 shows that those groups that have historically formed the nucleus of the Democratic party are under-represented in their party's most important decision-making process. In 1972 eleven of the thirteen socioeconomic groups with disproportionately Democratic party iden-tification were under-represented in the primary. An identical analysis for 1968 shows a similar finding. Of the eight socioeconomic groups under-represented that year, all eight were disproportionately Demo-cratic.

As evidenced by both the 1972 and 1968 California experience, the core of the Democratic party is comprised of one well-defined segment of American society, but the party's nomination process, instead of re-warding this support, bestows disproportionate influence on groups whose partisanship is significantly less Democratic.

Although these findings might disturb anyone either generally con-cerned about democracy and representation, or specifically concerned about Democratic party politics, it must be remembered that the focus so far has been only on demographic characteristics. A strong argument could be made that demographic unrepresentativeness, its severity and pervasiveness notwithstanding, is irrelevant as long as ideology, issue concerns, and, more importantly, candidate preferences are unrelated to, or independent of, the socioeconomic status of Democrats. For example, if 30 percent of all lower-class Democrats, middle-class Demo-crats, and upper-class Democrats considered themselves strongly con-servative, thought crime and national defense were the country's most pressing problems, and chose Hubert Humphrey as their presidential nominee, and if the remaining 70 percent of each social class called themselves liberal, thought pollution and conservation were the most pressing problems, and favored George McGovern, then variations in turnout and demographic unrepresentativeness were politically incon-

Table 3
Partisanship and Representation by Demographic Characteristics

1972 CALIFORNIA PRIMARY			1968 CALIFORNIA PRIMARY		
Education			*Education*		
8th grade and under	−	D	8th grade and under	−	D
9th–11th grade	−	D	9th–11th grade	−	D
High school	−	D	High school	−	D
1–3 years college	+	R	1–2 years college	+	R
College degree	+	R	3–4 years college	+	R
Advanced col. deg.	+	R	Advanced col. deg.	+	R
Income			*Income*		
Under $3,000	−	D	Under $3,000	−	D
$3,000–$6,999	−	D	$3,000–$6,999	−	D
$7,000–$9,999	−	D	$7,000–$9,999	*	D
$10,000–$14,999	+	D	$10,000–$14,999	+	R
$15,000–$19,999	+	R	Over $15,000	+	R
Over $20,000	+	R			
Social Class			*Social Class*		
Lower/lower mid	−	D	Lower/lower mid	−	D
Middle class	+	R	Middle class	+	D
Upper mid/upper	+	R	Upper mid/upper	+	R
Occupation			*Occupation*		
Blue-collar	−	D	Blue-collar	−	D
Sales/clerical	+	D	Sales/clerical	*	R
Exec/prof/mgr	+	R	Exec/prof/mgr	+	R
Race			*Race*		
White	+	R	White	+	R
Black	−	D	Black	*	D
Asian	−	D	Asian	*	D
Spanish	−	D	Spanish	−	D

SOURCE: California Polls 6804 and 7204, Field Research Corporation, San Francisco, Calif.

NOTE: D — Democratic party identification above the state average.
     R — Democratic party identification below the state average.
     + — Over-represented in primary.
     − — Under-represented in primary.
     * — Perfect representation.

sequential. The primary electorate would still faithfully reflect the rank and file's seventy to thirty split over ideology, issues, and candidates. These three empirical questions merit further consideration and are addressed in chapter 3.

NOTES

1. Party identification instead of party registration is used as a measure of party membership for two reasons. First, very little slippage exists. Of all Democratic party identifiers 93 percent said they were registered Democrats. Thus, as Appendix 1 shows, the effect on the findings is minimal. Second, party identification has advantages unique to the study of presidential primaries. It allows Democrats and Republicans to be identified in states which have no formal registration procedure, a consideration of special importance in states with open primaries. It also permits some citizens *not* to be Democrats and Republicans even though the registration system in their states forces them to choose a political party. In such states, the option to be "independent" is unavailable and party registration is presumably an inaccurate gauge of party membership. Democrats who willingly affiliate with the party and who should be included as party members cannot be differentiated from "independents" who were forced to register as Democrats.

In 1972, 51 percent (n=520) of the sample (N=1028) identified themselves as Democrats, and in 1968, 56 percent (n=718) of the sample (N=1294) did so. Both samples were apparently well drawn since these percentages correspond closely with official party registration figures for both years. Democratic Party registration was 56 percent in 1972 and 55 percent in 1968. *See* Eugene Lee and Bruce Keith, *California Votes, 1960-1972* (Berkeley: Institute of Governmental Studies, 1974), p. 27.

As is usually the case in California, Democratic turnout in both years was relatively high. In 1972, 66 percent (n=340) of all Democrats voted in their party's presidential primary; in 1968, 64 percent (n=460) voted. These turnout percentages, like those for registration, also support well-drawn samples. Democratic turnout in 1972 and 1968 were officially reported to be 64 and 66 percent respectively. *See Statement of Vote: State of California, 1972 Primary Election* (Sacramento: Secretary of State's Office, 1972) and *Statement of Vote: State of California, 1968 Primary Election* (Sacramento: Secretary of State's Office, 1968).

In 1972 eight Democrats (of the 520) did not answer whether they voted in the primary. Since they cannot be classified as either voters or nonvoters, they must be treated as missing data.

2. Sidney Verba and Norman H. Nie, *Participation in America: Political Democracy and Social Equality* (New York: Harper and Row, 1972), p. 96; Robert A. Dahl, *A Preface to Democratic Theory* (Chicago: University of Chicago Press, 1956), p. 114.

3. Although this measure is inferential and simple, it does require one word of caution. The amount of over-representation and under-representation is a function of both the percentage difference and the size of the group. For instance, a 4 percent difference in the proportion of blacks in the party membership and within the primary electorate constitutes an enormous disproportion because blacks comprise only 6 percent of the California Democratic party membership. A similar disproportion for males, who comprise almost 50 percent of all Democrats, produces a much smaller disproportion.

4. Field's surveys ask for the occupation of the head-of-household. A few of the occupational categories could not be used because Field coded into one category two or more occupations which usually exhibit differing behavioral or attitudinal tendencies. For instance, students and the unemployed formed one category. Since students and the unemployed do not necessarily share similar political dispositions it would make little sense to use this category.

5. In both 1968 and 1972 Field combined the objective measures of education, income, and occupation with a subjective assessment by the interviewer, and coded each respondent into one of ten categories: (1) lower class, (2) lower class, (3) lower middle class, (4) lower middle class, (5) middle class, (6) middle class, (7) middle class, (8) upper middle class, (9) upper middle class, (10) upper class.

In order to increase the "n" within each class, but still retain Field's original measure, I reduced his ten-point scale to the following four-point scale: (1) lower class, (1,2); (2) lower middle class (3,4); (3) middle class (5,6,7); and (4) upper middle/upper class (8,9,10).

6. Angus Campbell et al., *The American Voter* (New York: John Wiley and Sons, 1964), pp. 250–65; Verba and Nie, *Participation in America*, pp. 95–101, 125–37; V. O. Key, *Politics, Parties, and Pressure Groups*, 5th ed. (New York: Thomas Y. Crowell Co., 1964), pp. 585–86; Raymond E. Wolfinger and Steven J. Rosenstone, *Who Votes?* (New Haven, Conn.: Yale University Press, 1980).

7. These data are computed from the Center for Political Studies' national election studies for the indicated years.

8. Campbell et al., *American Voter*, pp. 49–64; Paul Lazarsfeld, Bernard Berelson, and Hazel Gaudet, *The People's Choice*, 3d ed. (New York: Columbia University Press, 1948), pp. 40–51.

9. Robert A. Dahl, ed., *Political Oppositions in Western Democracies* (New Haven: Yale University Press, 1966); Leon D. Epstein, *Political Parties in Western Democracies* (New York: Frederick A. Praeger, 1967); David E. Butler and Donald Stokes, *Political Change in Britain* (New York: St. Martin's Press, 1969); Seymour M. Lipset and Stein Rokkan, *Party Systems and Voter Alignments: Cross National Perspectives* (New York: Free Press, 1967); Giuseppe Di Palma, ed., *Mass Politics in Industrial Societies* (Chicago: Markham, 1972).

10. Robert R. Alford, "Class Voting in Anglo-American Political Systems," in Lipset and Rokkan, eds., *Party Systems and Voter Alignments*, pp. 67–93.

11. Erik Allardt and Pertti Pesonen, "Cleavages in Finnish Politics," in Lipset and Rokkan, eds., *Party Systems and Voter Alignments*, p. 342.

12. Juan J. Linz, "Cleavage and Consensus in West German Politics," in Lipset and Rokkan, eds., *Party Systems and Voter Alignments*, p. 286.

13. Fred I. Greenstein, *The American Party System and the American People* (Englewood Cliffs, N.J.: Prentice-Hall, 1970), pp. 23–25.

14. For corresponding data on national partisanship in 1972 *see* Frank J. Sorauf, *Party Politics in America*, 3d ed. (Boston: Little, Brown and Co., 1976), p. 152.

3

IDEOLOGY, ISSUE-CONCERNS, AND CANDIDATE PREFERENCES OF THE RANK AND FILE

> *The effective primary constituency ... may come to consist predominantly of ... people especially responsive to certain ... shades of ideology. ... or styles of political leadership.*
>
> V. O. Key

MUCH HAS been spoken and written about the ideology and issue-orientation of American political parties. And, as usual, opinion differs. To some, the Democratic and Republican parties resemble identical twins, mirror images of each other differing only in name. Adherents of this view claim that little ideological difference separates the parties at the elite level, and that this similarity at the top is projected into the party's candidates for office, its campaign platforms, and its policy positions. In fact, the exact difference between the parties has been carefully estimated to be less than a dime's worth, a measure quite appropriate for economics, but hardly fitting for political science.

An important correlate to the argument of ideologically sterile parties is the presence of an ideologically fertile electorate. Subscription to this belief has led more than one politician to run an ideologically based campaign in the hope of rallying that ideologically predisposed majority into electoral victory. But as the magnitudes of Goldwater's defeat in 1964, or Wallace's defeat in 1968, or McGovern's defeat in 1972 illustrate, pure conservatism, pure populism, and pure liberalism, as dished out by these three candidates, proved highly unappetizing to an overwhelming majority of voters. Candidates espousing a return to the "invisible hand" of Adam Smith were rejected just as resoundingly as candidates advocating the "good hands of All-State."

Despite the unimpeachable testimony of these three elections, the electoral myth carried over into 1976. This time Eugene McCarthy and Ronald Reagan hoped to capitalize on that elusive majority. To the surprise of few, their efforts proved just as fruitless as their predecessors'.

The third-party candidacy of Eugene McCarthy failed to receive 1 percent of the national presidential vote, and Ronald Reagan failed to receive his party's nomination.

Figures 4 and 5 show this commonly accepted view of the elite and the electorate. As the identical solid lines in figures 4 and 5 show, the perception of party elites remains the same regardless of party identification. Both Republican and Democratic adherents of the Tweedledum/ Tweedledee theory of American political parties see virtually no difference in the ideological and issue orientation at their party's elite level. On the other hand, the perception of the masses varies sharply by party. For Republicans, figure 4 accurately describes the ideological leaning of the masses; for Democrats, figure 5, the polar opposite, does the same job.

A more common perception of ideological dispositions in the United States, and one that has the backing of much empirical research, holds a contrary view—ideological differences between the parties are present at the elite level but nearly nonexistent at the mass level.[1] Figure 6 displays this view. Both parties' leaderships tend to be more ideologically distant (the Democratic elite, more liberal; the Republican elite, more conservative) than their party's supporters.

Although these three models are ideal types which may or may not conform to reality on any given issue or in any given election, they still remain the most common pictorial notion of our political parties, and thus, in spite of their oversimplification, retain substantial influence over actual behavior in the political sphere. If figure 4 fits party leaders' perceptions of the general population, then those leaders can easily see the types of candidates, the types of strategies, and the types of issues which their party should pursue to win elections. On the other hand, if figure 5 best describes the ideological disposition of the electorate, then a party should encourage and support quite different candidacies and issue stances, candidacies like those of George McGovern and Eugene McCarthy.

In the past when both parties' elites still controlled the national conventions, presidential nominees were intentionally chosen in response to such ideological perceptions of the party rank and file. Most often, both sides operated with figure 6 in mind. Occasionally, the Republicans opted for figure 4 and the Democrats for figure 5. With the extensive increase in presidential primaries this situation has changed. Primaries, unlike elites, cannot "perceive." They can only mirror. And they can only mirror the ideological dispositions of that share of the party membership which is actually reflected in the primary electorate. Thus, a question arises whether the demographic bias found in the California primaries also produced an ideological bias. For if groups that voted

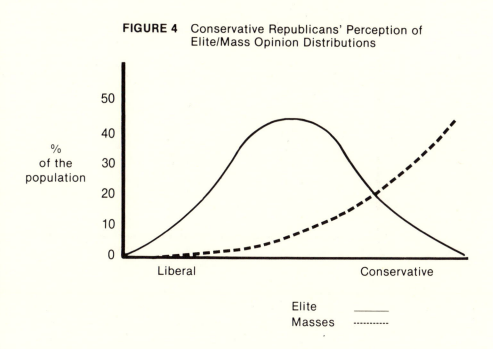

FIGURE 4 Conservative Republicans' Perception of Elite/Mass Opinion Distributions

%
of the
population

Liberal   Conservative

Elite   _____
Masses   ----------

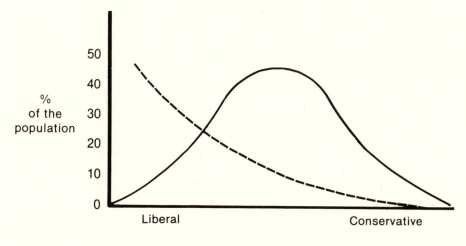

FIGURE 5 Liberal Democrats' Perception of Elite/Mass Opinion Distributions

%
of the
population

Liberal   Conservative

Elite   _____
Masses   ----------

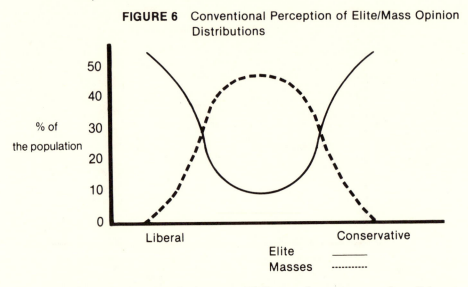

FIGURE 6   Conventional Perception of Elite/Mass Opinion Distributions

possessed ideological dispositions different from groups that did not, then primaries became (and become) institutionalized distorters, rather than recorders, of rank-and-file ideological leanings. In order to make such a determination, we must explore the possibility that ideology and issue-concerns within the California Democratic party were also socioeconomically related.

Most of the research on this crucial question, especially for the Democratic party, is found in the realignment literature. In fact, the common denominator of most realignment scenarios is the dissolution of the New Deal coalition within the Democratic party. Because of irreconcilable ideological perspectives and issue-concerns, intense factions (usually designated New Politics, New Deal, and Southern), each with their own mass constituency, brand of ideology, and set of candidate loyalties, will find compromise impossible. Eventually, developers of realignment scenarios say, the party system must head in one of three directions: first, disintegration of the Democratic coalition followed by a recoalescence around new issues and constituents into a revitalized majority party;[2] second, disintegration followed by realignment into a revitalized Republican majority;[3] or third, disintegration accompanied by either increased nonpartisanship or total anomie.[4]

Unrepresentativeness in primary electorates has important implications for hypothesized realignment. If intense factionalism does plague a party, and if the nomination process continually gives disproportionate power and perhaps, ultimately, control to one faction (and hence, to the interests, policies, issues, and candidates which that subgroup supports) then unrepresentativeness could hasten or hinder realignment, depending on its direction, pervasiveness, and severity. Factions, finding themselves comparatively disadvantaged and continually neglected in the nomination process, might begin to look for a new home elsewhere, and might conceivably find it in a more hospitable Republican party.

Fortunately, Field's data allow us to pursue this area of inquiry.[5] Each respondent in Field's survey was asked his ideological identification. The variable consisted of the usual five-category scale: strongly liberal, mildly liberal, middle-of-the-road, mildly conservative, and strongly conservative. Figure 7 presents the ideological composition of the California Democratic rank and file.

Figure 7 offers two interesting findings. First, the distribution of ideological identification within the California Democratic party much more closely resembles the normal distribution of figure 6 than the skewed distributions of either figure 4 or figure 5. The bulk of the party (81 percent) is either mildly ideological or middle-of-the-road, with only 19 percent at the extremes. There are no indications in figure 7 of a hidden ideological majority on either the right or the left. California thus conforms to the traditional model.

Second, as evidenced by the slightly bimodal distribution, the Democratic party in California does suffer from a mild ideological split. While

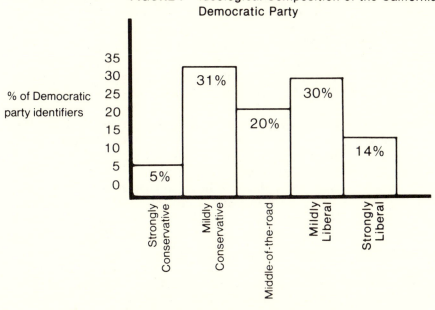

FIGURE 7 Ideological Composition of the California Democratic Party

Source: California Poll 7204, Field Research Corporation, San Francisco, Calif.

80 percent of the rank and file place themselves off of dead center in the ideological spectrum, 36 percent are conservative, and 44 percent are liberal. It is important to note that the split is between moderates, not extremists. Mildly conservative Democrats, the largest contingent, compose 31 percent of the party and 86 percent of the conservatives. Mildly liberal Democrats compose 30 percent of the party and 68 percent of the liberals. Thus, within the California Democratic party, neither ideology predominates. Both are embraced but embraced by the rank and file in moderation.

Given this ideological portrait, the next question is whether ideology differs by socioeconomic status within the party. Because all variables presented here are clearly correlated with education, and because of the magnitude of educational unrepresentativeness in both primaries, this analysis is limited to ideological and issue differences among Democrats by educational level. Table 4 cross-tabulates ideological self-identification of Democrats by education in 1972.

As table 4 shows, ideology and education were strongly related. The top row shows a sharp, linear drop in the percentage of conservative and middle-of-the-road Democrats as education increases.[6] Of all Democrats with an eighth-grade education or less 76 percent identified themselves as either conservative or middle-of-the-road. Among Democrats with a high school education, a college degree, and an advanced college degree, the percentage of conservative/middle-of-the-roaders drops to 47 percent, 37 percent, and 17 percent, respectively. Conversely, the number of liberal Democrats dramatically increases with education. Only 24 percent of all Democrats with an eighth-grade education or less and 32 percent of all Democrats with a high school diploma chose the liberal label. In contrast, 63 percent of all college-educated Democrats, and 83 percent of all advanced-degree Democrats classified themselves in that way.

Table 5 shows ideology and education similarly related in 1968. The most conservative and middle-of-the-road groups were Democrats with a high school education or less; the most liberal were Democrats with some college experience or more.[7]

Viewed in conjunction with the findings in chapter 2, tables 4 and 5 suggest that primaries have a great potential for ideological distortion. The California Democratic party was evenly split between liberals and conservatives, but socioeconomic characteristics of Democrats were strongly related to both ideology and turnout. As a result, the voice of the party faithful, as transmitted through presidential primaries, assumed a sharp ideological accent. In both years, the high turnout/over-represented groups were also the most liberal groups within the party. In contrast, the most under-represented—and I might add, Democratically partisan—groups were also the most conservative/middle-of-the-road elements within the party.

Table 4

Ideological Self-Identification of Democrats by Education—1972

	8TH & UNDER	9-11	HIGH SCHOOL	1-3 COLLEGE	COLLEGE DEGREE	ADVANCED DEGREE
Con/m of r[a]	76%	72%	68%	47%	37%	17%
Liberal	24%	28%	32%	53%	63%	83%
	100%	100%	100%	100%	100%	100%
n =	42	64	157	144	46	42

SOURCE: California Poll 7204, Field Research Corporation, San Francisco, Calif.

[a]Conservative and middle-of-the-road

Table 5

Ideological Self-Identification of Democrats by Education—1968

	8TH & UNDER	9-11	HIGH SCHOOL	1-3 COLLEGE	COLLEGE DEGREE	ADVANCED DEGREE
Con/m of r[a]	76%	69%	69%	60%	43%	41%
Liberal	24%	31%	31%	40%	57%	59%
	100%	100%	100%	100%	100%	100%
n =	86	106	226	122	68	29

SOURCE: California Poll 6804, Field Research Corporation, San Francisco, Calif.
[a]Conservative and middle-of-the-road

Table 6
Strength of Ideological Conviction by Educational Level of Democrats—1972

	8TH & UNDER	9-11	HIGH SCHOOL	1-3 COLLEGE	COLLEGE DEGREE	ADVANCED DEGREE
Strong conservative	2%	13%	6%	2%	4%	5%
Moderate	95%	78%	85%	81%	78%	55%
Strong liberal	2%	9%	9%	17%	17%	41%
	99%	100%	100%	100%	99%	101%
n =	42	64	157	144	46	42

SOURCE: California Poll 7204, Field Research Corporation, San Francisco, Calif.
NOTE: Columns do not add up to 100% due to rounding.

The analysis can be extended to determine whether strength of ideological conviction was also related to education. In order to isolate the strong ideologues, the five-category ideological self-identification scale was combined into three categories: strongly liberal, moderate (which combined the mildly liberal, middle-of-the-road, and mildly conservative categories), and strongly conservative. The data are presented in table 6.[8]

As the absence of any pattern in the top line indicates, strongly conservative self-identification was unrelated to education. Nearly identical proportions of Democrats with a high school education (6 percent), college degree (4 percent), and advanced college degree (5 percent) thought of themselves as strongly conservative.

As the bottom line indicates, however, the same cannot be said of strongly liberal convictions. Whereas only 2 percent of all Democrats with an eighth-grade education or less chose the strongly liberal label, 17 percent of all Democrats with some college experience, and 41 percent of all Democrats with an advanced college degree considered themselves strongly liberal. Thus, in addition to upsetting the party's ideological balance by advantaging liberal elements, primaries distorted the party's moderate ideological character by advantaging liberal extremists.

Regardless of the care with which they are done, ideological analyses suffer certain problems, two of which occur here. First, because ideology is subjectively rather than objectively measured, the labels may be either meaningless to the respondents (that is, void of any coherent and consistent pattern of political beliefs and attitudes) or descriptive of a highly integrated philosophy guiding the respondent's *personal*, but not *political*, behavior. Second, the presence of ideological differences, even if cognitively rooted in political issues, does not mean that Democrats vote for nominees according to those same standards. The rank and file may be unable to perceive issue or ideological differences among the candidates, or other factors, such as charisma or style, may override issue or ideological considerations. Because of the possibility that one or another of these caveats might modify the findings of ideological distinction, they are examined at greater length in the next two sections.

ISSUE DIFFERENCES WITHIN THE CALIFORNIA DEMOCRATIC PARTY

Presidential primaries are more than just popularity contests between political candidates. Because they offer the party rank and file an opportunity to voice their opinions about the issues of the day, they also take on the characteristics of referenda as well. If George McGovern wins primary after primary and, ultimately, the Democratic party's presidential nomination, on a platform of liberal economic policy, permissive social policy, and isolationist foreign policy, then his victory will be interpreted as indicating rank-and-file support for, or endorsement of, these positions. In response, other party leaders will surely try to redirect party policy in these directions, and other candidates with similar track records will be lured into the party's future nomination contests. If primary electorates accurately reflect rank-and-file issue-concerns, then these adjustments make the party more responsive to changing conditions and are, in fact, indicative of a healthy and functioning democratic society. On the other hand, if the issue-concerns of the party's membership are distorted by the primary electorate, then resulting elite adjustments may mean defeat for the party in the short run (in the November election) or even permanent realignment (of both parties) around different issues and constituents in the long run.

As shown in chapter 2, primary electorates were demographically unrepresentative of the party rank and file and this demographic bias might also have produced an issue bias if demographic characteristics and issue-concerns were also strongly related.

It is at least conceivable that issue-concerns varied little among different socioeconomic groups which made up the Democratic party. All had, after all, freely decided to call themselves Democrats and that identity could have led to a consensus on issue-concerns within the party.

A little reflection, however, suggests that this will never be more than a straw-man argument. First, different socioeconomic backgrounds produce different life experiences, and those, in turn, presumably create different images of the outside world. Second, these "mind sets" are present long before most individuals choose their party identification and are in any case rooted in basic, primary groups rather than in reference groups chosen on an associational basis. Third, and in extension of the second point, values, issue-concerns, and attitudes rarely determine choice of party; instead, offspring tend to adopt the party identification of their parents, regardless of the affinity (or lack thereof) between personal beliefs and party policy.[9] In short, a party label seems unlikely to undo twenty years or more of primary group programming.

Of course, to check the validity of either explanation, it needs to be put to the empirical test. The California poll data allows us to make such a test. In 1972 Mervin Field asked his respondents what two or three issues were most important to them. The exact question was "Here is a list of some issues which the presidential candidates are talking about. All are important, but which two or three do you think are of the utmost importance to you?" The complete list of issues was: controlling air and water pollution; conserving natural resources; reducing crime and violence; extending and improving social welfare programs; providing jobs/education/housing for minorities; reducing drug and narcotic use; reducing taxes; controlling inflation; providing jobs; improving relations with foreign countries; extending and improving the military defense; and improving racial integration.

Probably the hottest issue of 1972, if it is extrapolated from George McGovern's sudden emergence into the national limelight, was the Vietnam War. Strong antiwar sentiment was purported to be responsible for McGovern's strong showing against Edmund Muskie in the New Hampshire Democratic presidential primary; McGovern's subsequent victory in Wisconsin, the one which turned him into a presidential nominee, was said to confirm that wisdom. If we can believe these primary outcomes as filtered through their interpreters, the party membership wanted not just a new face, but a face with antiwar features.

At first glance, this might also explain McGovern's later primary victory in California. Table 7 presents the frequency distribution of the most important problem question, and as the table shows, "ending the war in Vietnam" was the most important issue-concern of California Democrats. In fact, a majority (58 percent) of all Democrats picked the war as one of their three most important issues.[10]

Whether the priority of this issue (Vietnam) and the victory of one candidate (McGovern) can be linked in simple mandate fashion is less

Table 7
Frequency Distribution of Most Important Problems for Democratic Party Identifiers—1972

	%	N
Ending the war	58%	229
Pollution	37%	192
Jobs	33%	169
Inflation	28%	144
Taxes	24%	125
Drugs	22%	116
Crime	21%	109
Conservation	14%	72
Assisting minorities	14%	71
Improving education	13%	68
Racial integration	13%	66
Welfare	8%	40
Defense programs	5%	28
Foreign relations	4%	20

SOURCE: California Poll 7204, Field Research Corporation, San Francisco, Calif.

clear.[11] The Vietnam issue itself is partly responsible for muddying the question. There was in fact support for ending the war through annihilation, escalation, negotiation, disengagement, and surrender. Unfortunately, Field's question failed to distinguish between these solutions, leaving hawks, doves, and other birds of prey and peace lumped together in the 58 percent who favored "ending the war." What is more critical, however, is whether the percentage of Democrats who favored ending the war varied by socioeconomic status, thereby creating a primary electorate more concerned about ending the war, and hence, the war candidate, than the party membership as a whole. Table 8 cross-tabulates "ending the war" in Vietnam by the educational level of Democrats.

As table 8 shows, concern over ending the war was not equally shared among California Democrats, but was strongly associated with education—the less educated, the less concerned; the better educated, the more concerned. Only 44 percent of all Democrats with an eighth-grade education or less and 46 percent of all Democrats with a ninth-to-eleventh grade education mentioned the war as one of the country's three most important problems. In comparison, an overwhelming concern was shown by the Democratic educational elite. Seventy-six percent of all Democrats with a college degree, and 79 percent of all Democrats with an advanced college degree chose the war as one of their three most important problems.

Demographically related differences over issues were not just limited to Vietnam. Table 9 shows that other issues in 1972 also pitted the educational elite within the Democratic party against their less-educated counterparts. Less-educated Democrats were proportionately more concerned about social issues (crime, taxes, drugs) and, to a lesser extent, about aid to minorities and the U.S. international position (foreign relations and military defense). On the other hand, better-educated Democrats tended to be more concerned about conservation, pollution, and, as well they might be, education. Although the differences are not as large as were the responses to the question about Vietnam, they are clear and they form a pattern consistent with our earlier findings which showed lower-status Democrats holding down one set of positions on the ideological continuum and upper-status Democrats holding down another.

For yet a third set of issues, variations in turnout mean little because of the U-shaped and ∩-shaped distributions of these opinions within the party. U-shaped distributions emerge when concern for a particular issue is concentrated at both extremes of the educational continuum; ∩-shaped distributions, when concern is concentrated in the middle. Little advantage or disadvantage is bestowed upon the issue, its

Table 8
"Ending the War" by Educational Level of Democrats—1972

	8TH & UNDER	9-11	HIGH SCHOOL	1-3 COL	3 COL	COL DEGREE	ADVANCED DEGREE
Mentioned ending war	44%	46%	54%	58%	68%	76%	79%
Did not mention	56%	54%	46%	42%	32%	24%	21%
	100%	100%	100%	100%	100%	100%	100%
n =	52	68	162	124	25	46	43

SOURCE: California Poll 7204, Field Research Corporation, San Francisco, Calif.

Table 9
Most Important Problems by Educational Level of Democrats—1972

	UNDER HIGH SCHOOL	HIGH SCHOOL	1–3 COL	COL DEGREE	ADVANCED DEGREE
Crime & violence	26%	23%	20%	20%	7%
Taxes	32%	27%	21%	20%	7%
Drugs & narcotics	25%	27%	22%	17%	5%
Jobs/educ/ housing for minorities	18%	13%	12%	13%	12%
Foreign relations	6%	3%	4%	2%	2%
Military defense	5%	7%	5%	2%	2%
Pollution	32%	36%	43%	30%	42%
Education	11%	10%	13%	22%	23%
Conservation	10%	8%	17%	17%	30%
Welfare	11%	6%	5%	9%	14%
Jobs	26%	39%	34%	30%	26%
Inflation	25%	25%	30%	35%	28%
Racial integration	11%	10%	16%	11%	19%

SOURCE: California Poll 7204, Field Research Corporation, San Francisco, Calif.

spokesmen, and its followers by either distribution since high turnout among better-educated Democrats compensates for, or cancels, the low turnout of their less-educated brethren. Turnout among the middle-educational groups tends to fall not just between the two extremes but around the mean for the state as a whole.

From table 9 we see that support for extending welfare was essentially U-shaped. What concern there was over this issue is located among the least-educated Democrats, presumably because they are the recipients of welfare payments, and among the best-educated, perhaps because of feelings of noblesse oblige. Those Democrats with the least to gain from welfare and the most to lose, middle Americans, were less supportive. On the other hand, issues such as controlling inflation and providing jobs fit the ∩-shaped distribution. Here, concern was concentrated in the middle educational levels and tailed off to either end. Possibly because the jobs of those in the middle are most affected by ups and downs in the economy, there is a higher concern among such Democrats. Again, however, because their turnout approximates the state mean, and because turnout at the extremes is offsetting, issues with this type of distribution tend to be fairly well represented in primary electorates.

In his post-primary survey of 1968, the fourth in a series of polls conducted that year, and the one used in this study, Mervin Field did not include the most important problem question. As a result, the preceeding analysis cannot be duplicated for that particular sample. However, he did ask it one month later in his fifth survey, and the findings are still useful for demonstrating the stability of these issue patterns within the party across time.

Table 10 presents the frequency distribution for the most important problem of Democratic party identifiers in 1968 and, although issue and

Table 10
Frequency Distribution of Most Important
Problems for Democratic Party Identifiers—
1968

	%	N
Vietnam	54%	304
Crime and violence	31%	172
Taxes	19%	107
Inflation	18%	100
Equal opportunity/Blacks	13%	72
Problems of poor	11%	62
Education	11%	61
Providing jobs	9%	52
Problems of young people	8%	46
Dealing with Russia	8%	42
Medical care	5%	30
National defense	5%	28
Draft	5%	26
Problems of elderly	4%	23
Dealing with China	2%	13

SOURCE: California Poll 6805, Field Research Corporation, San Francisco, Calif.

question wording differ, a certain continuity and stability can be discerned for both years. In 1968 concern about Vietnam again ranked highest with a little better than one out of every two Democrats (54 percent) choosing the war as their most important concern. Following Vietnam, in order of importance, were crime (31 percent), taxes (19 percent), inflation (18 percent), and federal assistance to minorities (11 percent). Comparing tables 9 and 10 we see that four of the five top issues in 1968 (Vietnam, crime, taxes, and inflation) reappeared as top issues four years later.

Since the passage of time permits some issues to persist, others to die, some to appear, and others to reappear, the congruity or lack of congruity among issues over time is only an interesting sidelight to the more important question of the ways concern with such issues is distinguished within the party rank and file. Given the role of primaries as transmitters of rank-and-file opinion, the continual over-representation of certain elements within the party, (if they possess issue-concerns different from those who are under-represented) may in fact determine why some issues persist, die, appear, or reappear. Therefore, an examination of issue differences within the party in 1968 will help to determine whether the findings in 1972 were a unique chapter in Democratic electoral politics or part of a continuing drama played out year after year.

Table 11 cross-tabulates concern over the Vietnam War in 1968 with the educational level of Democrats. Scanning the top row we see that in 1968, as in 1972, concern over the war was not equally shared among California Democrats, but was again strongly related to education. Less-educated Democrats were less concerned about the war; better-educated Democrats, more concerned. Of all Democrats with an eighth-grade education or less, only 37 percent mentioned the war as one of the problems about which they were most concerned. At the highest educational level, 69 percent of all Democrats chose it.

Internal differences over issues were not just limited to Vietnam. By

Table 11
Concern over Vietnam War by Educational Level of Democrats—1968

	8TH & UNDER	9–11	HIGH SCHOOL	1–2 COL	3–4 COL	ADVANCED DEGREE
Mentioned Vietnam	37%	55%	54%	60%	58%	69%
Did not mention	63%	45%	46%	40%	42%	31%
	100%	100%	100%	100%	100%	100%
n =	73	100	208	84	57	35

SOURCE: California Poll 6805, Field Research Corporation, San Francisco, Calif.

approximately two to one margins, Democrats with a high school degree or less were more concerned about taxes (21 percent to 9 percent), inflation (19 percent to 6 percent), medical care (7 percent to 3 percent), jobs (10 percent to 6 percent), crime (33 percent to 17 percent), and problems of the elderly (6 percent to 0 percent). In contrast, and by nearly the same margin, better-educated Democrats were more concerned about racial integration (34 percent to 10 percent) and, again, education (17 percent to 10 percent).

It is readily apparent from the turnout, ideology, and issue data that differences exist among California Democrats. Some groups possess one type of behavioral and attitudinal pattern, others possess another. It is also just as apparent that since ideology, issues, and turnout are similarly related to socioeconomic background, primaries act as a magnifying glass rather than a mirror. Certain constituents and interests are reflected through the concave side of the glass; other groups and interests suffer reflection through the convex side.

PREFERENTIAL DIFFERENCES WITHIN THE CALIFORNIA DEMOCRATIC PARTY

Up to this point, primaries have been treated solely in the context of their role as communicators of opinion between the party elite and party rank and file, and the findings have been discussed in terms of their effects on the substance of that communication. But primaries are much more than party opinion surveys. They are a method by which parties select their nominees and, as such, they raise the question of whether candidate preferences, regardless of reason (style, issues, ideology), are also related to demographic characteristics and, hence, subject to the distortive effects of primaries. If unrelated, the election outcome will remain unaffected by variations in turnout, and each candidate's strength will be accurately reflected in the primary electorate. In such a case, unrepresentativeness remains theoretically interesting, but is of much less practical political significance.

Two methods were available to determine whether the candidate preferences of Democrats were demographically related. The first alternative was to use the post-primary survey and to examine the candidate preferences of Democratic voters by socioeconomic background. But using candidate vote as a measure of preference offers no way, short of inference, to measure the preference of nonvoters. That is, if less-educated (Democratic) voters preferred one candidate over another, can the same candidate preference be attributed to less-educated nonvoters? This inference is probably quite reasonable, but the absence of corroborative evidence still makes it tentative. The second alternative was to use a pre-election survey and examine the candidate preferences of all

FIGURE 8   Candidate Preferences of Democratic Party
Identifiers by Education
(1972 Pre-Election Survey)

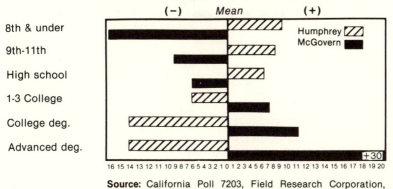

Source: California Poll 7203, Field Research Corporation,
San Francisco, Calif.

Democratic identifiers. Since candidate preferences were asked of
everyone, inferences would be unnecessary.

Fortunately, instead of having to choose and defend one approach, I
could use both, although I was limited to the first approach in 1968. As
the reader will quickly discern from figures 8, 9, and 10, both measures
yielded identical findings.

The graphs, set to a mean of "0" to facilitate comparisons between
candidates across time, show candidate preference strongly related to
the educational level of the Democratic rank and file before the 1972
primary and candidate choice strongly related to the educational level of
1972 and 1968 Democratic primary voters. By margins ranging from 12 to

FIGURE 9   Candidate Choice of Democratic Primary Voters by
Education (1972 Post-Election Survey)

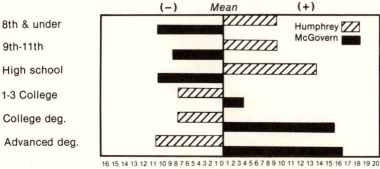

Source: California Polls 7204, Field Research Corporation,
San Francisco, Calif.

FIGURE 10   Candidate Choice of Democratic Primary Voters by Education (1968 Post-Election Survey)

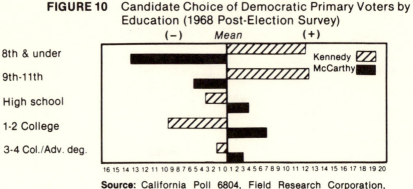

Source: California Poll 6804, Field Research Corporation, San Francisco, Calif.

25 percent, less-educated Democrats and Democratic voters preferred Hubert Humphrey in 1972 and Robert Kennedy in 1968. In striking contrast, by margins ranging from 8 percent to 32 percent, better-educated Democrats preferred McGovern and McCarthy in those same years.

Note the similarity between, first, Humphrey's and Kennedy's major sources of support within the party (figures 8, 9, and 10); second, the educational groups that are traditionally Democratic in party affiliation (figure 2); and third, the groups that are, due to low turnout (figure 3), underrepresented in primary electorates (table 2). The inverse comparisons can, of course, be made for McGovern's and McCarthy's sources of support.

Because education is related to other socioeconomic characteristics, these findings are not just limited to schooling, but permeate those other categories as well. In fact, of the thirteen socioeconomic groups under-represented in 1972, Hubert Humphrey was disproportionately preferred by ten (eighth grade and under, ninth to eleventh, high school, under $3,000, $3,000–$6,999, lower class, lower middle class, operatives/semi-skilled, craftsmen/skilled/foremen, and Asian/Hispanic). Of the eleven groups of Democrats over-represented in 1972, six preferred George McGovern (1-2 college, college degree, $10,000–$14,999, over $20,000, upper middle/upper class, professional/executive/managerial). Of the ten groups under-represented in 1968, nine favored Robert Kennedy (eighth and under, ninth to eleventh, under $3,000, $3,000–$6,999, lower class, lower middle class, laborers/service, operatives/semiskilled, and Asian/Hispanic). Of the ten groups of Democrats over-represented in 1968, nine favored Eugene McCarthy (1-2 college, advanced college degree, $10,000–14,999, over $15,000, middle class, upper middle/upper class, craftsmen/foremen/skilled, professional/executive/managerial, and white).

The pervasiveness of the findings and the inherent bias in the process is clearly illustrated when you compare the overlap in representation and candidate choice for all socioeconomic groups for both years. This has been done in table 12. Note the consistency and selectivity with which over-representation and under-representation bestowed their advantages and disadvantages on certain constituencies, and hence, on certain candidates, ideological perspectives, and issue-concerns. Of the ten socioeconomic groups of Democrats that were under-represented in both 1968 and 1972, and to which candidate preferences can be attached,

Table 12
Candidate Choice by Representation

CANDIDATE PREFERENCE	DEMOCRATS UNDER-REPRESENTED IN 1968 AND 1972	DEMOCRATS OVER-REPRESENTED IN 1968 AND 1972
Kennedy/Humphrey (1968) (1972)	8th & under 9th–11th grade Under $3,000 $3,000–$6,999 Lower class Lower middle class Operatives/semiskilled Service/household Asian/Hispanic	
Kennedy/McGovern (1968) (1972)		
McCarthy/Humphrey (1968) (1972)	High school	
McCarthy/McGovern (1968) (1972)		1–4 years college Advanced col. degree $10,000–$14,999 Over $15,000 Upper mid/upper class Prof/exec/mgr

SOURCE: California Polls 6804 and 7204, Field Research Corporation, San Francisco, Calif.

nine disproportionately preferred both Kennedy and Humphrey—the two more moderate candidates in both races. Of the six groups of Democrats that were over-represented in both elections, and to which disproportionate candidate choice can be attached, all six preferred Eugene McCarthy and George McGovern—the two liberal ideologues in both campaigns.

Chapter 3 serves a threefold purpose. First, it describes the patterns of opinions and candidate preferences that must exist within the Democratic party before variations in turnout, and hence, demographic unrepresentativeness can actually distort the ideological, attitudinal, and preferential character of the party's primary electorate. Second, it shows that those patterns were, in fact, present within the California Democratic party in 1968 and 1972. Third, it identifies the types of candidates and the types of issues that were advantaged and disadvantaged by the party's use of an electorally based nomination process. What the study fails to reveal, thus far, is just how much advantage these particular sets of relationships and distributions conferred upon those candidates. Chapter 4 will consider this question.

NOTES

1. Herbert McClosky, Paul J. Hoffmann, and Rosemary O'Hara, "Issue Conflict and Consensus among Party Leaders and Followers," *American Political Science Review* 54 (June 1960): 406–27; Jeane J. Kirkpatrick, "Representation in American National Conventions: The Case of 1972," *British Journal of Political Science* 5 (1975): 265–322; Philip E. Converse, "The Nature of Belief Systems in Mass Publics," in David E. Apter, ed., *Ideology and Discontent* (New York: Free Press, 1964), pp. 238–45; V. O. Key, *Public Opinion and American Democracy* (New York: Alfred A. Knopf, 1960), p. 179, pp. 432–57.

2. Lanny J. Davis, *The Emerging Democratic Majority* (New York: Stein and Day, 1974).

3. Kevin P. Phillips, *The Emerging Republican Majority* (New Rochelle, N.Y.: Arlington House, 1969).

4. For the nonpartisanship argument *see* Walter DeVries and Lance Tarrance, Jr., *The Ticket Splitter: A New Force in American Politics* (Grand Rapids: Eerdmans, 1972). For the anomie argument *see* Walter Dean Burnham, *Critical Elections and the Mainsprings of American Politics* (New York: W. W. Norton, 1970).

5. California Polls 6804 and 7204, Field Research Corporation, San Francisco, Calif.

6. The "conservative" and "middle-of-the-road" categories were combined because both were negatively related to education. The category "liberal" in table 4 combines the "mildly liberal" and "strongly liberal" categories.

7. The ideological self-identification question in 1968 had only three categories: liberal, middle-of-the-road, and conservative.

8. I cannot examine the same relationship in 1968 because the ideological self-identification variable in 1968 did not contain the two extreme categories.

9. M. Kent Jennings and Richard G. Niemi, *The Political Character of Adolescence: The Influence of Families and Schools* (Princeton: Princeton University Press, 1974), p. 41.

10. The total exceeds 100 percent because two or three "most important problems" were mentioned. Therefore the percentage is based on the total number of times a problem (i.e., ending the war) was mentioned (i.e., 299) divided by the total number of respondents (i.e., 520).

11. Inferring voters' opinions and positions from electoral outcomes is difficult to do. In 1968 Eugene McCarthy, campaigning on an antiwar platform, surprised the nation with a strong showing in the New Hampshire Democratic primary. At the time, the election was interpreted as a "peace vote." In fact, however, among McCarthy voters, hawks outnumbered doves by a three-to-two margin. *See* Philip E. Converse et al., "Continuity and Change in American Politics: Parties and Issues in the 1968 Election," *American Political Science Review* 63 (December 1969): 1090.

4

THE EFFECT OF UNREPRESENTATIVENESS: THE 1972 CALIFORNIA PRESIDENTIAL PRIMARY

TWO YARDSTICKS are available for measuring the worth of any academic area of inquiry. Some people, institutions, processes, and events are deemed important because of their intrinsic, historical worth, that is, their past or present impact on social, economic, and political life. Other areas merit study because an understanding of these events broadens our knowledge of other, similar types of events. In short, the greater the impact, or the greater the potential generality of the findings, the more worthy of investigation the object becomes in the eyes of the scholarly community.

Based solely on intrinsic, historical worth, and regardless of what it tells us about primaries in other states and at other electoral levels, the 1972 California primary surely deserves whatever serious attention students of American government can give. By permanently retiring one presidential contender (Hubert Humphrey) and by instantly crowning another (George McGovern), the 1972 primary emerged as an important historical variable that may have single-handedly shaped the course of recent political history. To wit: a different outcome in California might well have produced a different nominee. A different nominee, in turn, might have increased the level of competitiveness in the November general election. At worst, a more competitive general election might have reduced the size of the landslide. This, in turn, might have altered the victor's perception of his electoral mandate, and consequently, acted as a constraint on his subsequent behavior in office. At best, a more competitive Democratic nominee might have conceivably produced a different winner. That this change would have altered numerous events of the past decade requires little imagination.

Since turnout and candidate preferences were both related to the socioeconomic status of Democrats, McGovern's supporters were over-represented in the primary, and Humphrey's supporters were under-represented. What amount of this preferential unrepresentativeness was present in the electorate, and what impact, if any, may this have had on the final outcome?[1]

Ordinarily, measuring the effect of demographic unrepresentativeness on primary outcomes involves a simple mathematical calculation. First, a demographically representative primary electorate is reconstructed from the actual sample. Table 13 (Step 1) compares the actual educational composition of the 1972 primary electorate to the ideal educational composition that would have occurred given either universal or proportionally equal turnout.

Second, candidate preferences are apportioned within each educational subgroup in the "ideal" primary electorate according to the percentage that each candidate received from each educational subgroup in the actual primary electorate. Table 14 shows step two in the procedure.

Finally the number of votes for each candidate would then be totalled, expressed as a percentage of the total N, and compared to the outcome in the actual primary election. This comparison would show the net change in a candidate's percentage of the vote given a representative primary electorate.

Unfortunately, Field's California Poll data complicate matters considerably. Although his samples were well drawn—as indicated by the accuracy of his party registration, party identification, and turnout figures—they were not immune to a problem common to many post-election surveys: a bandwagon effect. Whether the reason was social or psychological, some respondents reported voting for the winner despite

Table 13

Step 1: Transformation of Educationally Unrepresentative Electorate into Educationally Representative Electorate

	ACTUAL		IDEAL	
	%	n	%	n
8th grade and under	9%	31	10%	34
9th–11th grade	9%	32	13%	44
High school	28%	96	31%	105
1–3 years college	30%	103	29%	99
College degree	12%	39	9%	31
Advanced college degree	12%	39	8%	27
	100%	340	100%	340

SOURCE: California Poll 7204, Field Research Corporation, San Francisco, Calif.
NOTE: *n* = number of respondents per category

Table 14
Step 2: Allocation of Candidate Vote

	CORRECTED n PER CATEGORY		ACTUAL CANDIDATE VOTE PER GROUP		CORRECTED n PER CANDIDATE
8th and under	(34)	×	(% for Humphrey)	=	(n for Humphrey)
	(34)	×	(% for McGovern)	=	(n for McGovern)
9th–11th grade	(44)	×	(% for Humphrey)	=	(n for Humphrey)
	(44)	×	(% for McGovern)	=	(n for McGovern)
High school	(105)	×	(% for Humphrey)	=	(n for Humphrey)
	(105)	×	(% for McGovern)	=	(n for McGovern)
1–3 college	(99)	×	(% for Humphrey)	=	(n for Humphrey)
	(99)	×	(% for McGovern)	=	(n for McGovern)
College degree	(31)	×	(% for Humphrey)	=	(n for Humphrey)
	(31)	×	(% for McGovern)	=	(n for McGovern)
Adv col deg	(27)	×	(% for Humphrey)	=	(n for Humphrey)
	(27)	×	(% for McGovern)	=	(n for McGovern)

Source: California Poll 7204, Field Research Corporation, San Francisco, Calif.

actually voting for the loser. Naturally, every vote subtracted from the loser's totals and added to the winner's totals, increases the margin of victory by two votes. According to official 1972 election returns, George McGovern received 44 percent of the vote, and Hubert Humphrey received 39 percent of the vote. The Field data, however, show McGovern receiving 55 percent of the vote, and Humphrey receiving 27 percent of the vote.

From the outset it is important to underline the fact that since the findings in chapter 2 are based on extremely accurate turnout, party identification, and party registration figures, they remain unaffected by this discrepancy in candidate preference. The "candidate preference" findings in chapter 3 are also unaffected, given the acceptance of reasonable assumptions.

If one assumes that more lower-SES (socioeconomic status) Democrats jumped on the bandwagon than upper-SES Democrats, then figure 9 actually underestimates Humphrey's support among lower-SES Democrats and overestimates McGovern's support. By diluting the strength of the relationship between candidate preference and socioeconomic status, the bandwagon effect thus contributes to an understatement of the severity of the problem, while removing any doubt about its actual presence and direction. On the other hand, if one assumes that equal proportions of Democrats from all walks of life "went with the winner," then of course the direction and strength of the reported relationship in figure 9 closely approximates the direction and strength of the actual relationship. Only if one assumes that the bandwagon effect centered predominantly or exclusively among upper-SES Democrats can one question the validity of the findings. This last possibility, however, seems highly unlikely for two reasons. First, upper-SES individuals are less susceptible to minor social or psychological pressures to conform. Second, and even more convincing, the pre-election survey (figure 8) shows upper-SES Democrats already in the winner's column prior to the election.

The presence of a bandwagon does, however, create a problem when trying to measure the amount of preferential unrepresentativeness. Fortunately, the problem is not insurmountable. By assuming the presence of a bandwagon, and by identifying its pattern, one is able to correct for the problem in the sample. Once the effect has been eliminated from the sample, we can then proceed with the above-mentioned calculation of preferential unrepresentativeness.[2]

Table 15 compares the official outcome of the 1972 Democratic presi-

Table 15
Official Results of California Democratic Primary
Versus Survey Results, 1972

CANDIDATE	OFFICIAL RESULTS	SURVEY RESULTS
George McGovern	44%	55%
Hubert Humphrey	39%	27%
George Wallace[a]	8%	8%
Shirley Chisholm	4%	3%
Edmund Muskie	2%	3%
Sam Yorty	1%	1%
Eugene McCarthy	1%	1%
Others	2%	3%
	101%[b]	101%[b]

SOURCE: California Poll 7204, Field Research Corporation, San Francisco, Calif.; *Presidential Elections Since 1789* (Washington, D.C.: Congressional Quarterly, Inc., 1979), p. 167.

[a] Write-in
[b] Due to rounding

dential primary to the results found in Mervin Field's survey. A close
look at table 15 shows that reasonable assumptions can, in fact, be made
about the presence, direction, and number of "jumpers."

The first point worth noting is that the votes of only two candidates,
the first- and second-place finishers, are affected. That only the winner's
(McGovern's) totals increased adds credence to the belief that this discrepancy is a product of a bandwagon rather than a biased sample. That
the bandwagon would draw exclusively from the second-place finisher
(Humphrey) also seems reasonable since the first- and second-place
candidates accounted for 83 percent of the total vote. In addition, Humphrey's support centered among those groups within the Democratic
party who might succumb more easily to this type of social and
psychological pressure. No other candidate, including George Wallace
and Shirley Chisholm, appealed so strongly to lower-SES voters. Wallace's vote centered predominantly among middle-Americans (the middle educational, income, and occupational categories) and tapered off
among Americans at both ends of the SES spectrum. Chisholm's support, on the other hand, was concentrated among better-educated,
higher-income blacks.

The absence of a bandwagon effect among the supporters of the fringe
candidates is also not surprising. Wallace supporters, for instance, who
were hell-bent on "sending them a message," and who had to take the
time and the effort to write Wallace's name on their ballots, were not
about to abandon him in an interview situation. The strength of their
candidate loyalty would have far outweighed any social or psychological
pressures to defect after the primary, and, in fact, the survey situation
itself might have been interpreted as another golden opportunity for
sending that message.

The same reasoning can be applied to the few supporters of the other
candidates. It takes extremely strong candidate loyalties or extreme dis-
taste for the possible winners, to support a candidate who has no chance
whatsoever of winning, and who, because of winner-take-all delegate
allocations, has no chance of even picking up delegates to the national
convention. Very few voters who stuck by their candidates in this type
of hopeless situation would have abandoned him in a post-election
interview.

The second point that should be noted from table 15 is that there exists
a one-to-one relationship in the vote discrepancy of the first and second
place finishers. Humphrey's percentage of the vote dropped by 11½
percentage points, and McGovern's percentage increased by the same
margin. An 11½ percentage-point difference represents a shift of
thirty-nine voters in the sample. When the sample is corrected for this
shift or bandwagon effect, each candidate's percentage of the survey

vote will equal his percentage of the primary vote. That is, by subtracting 11½ percentage points (or 39 votes) from McGovern's total (55% − 11½% = 43½%, or rounded, 44%), and by adding 11½ percentage points (or 39 votes) to Humphrey's totals (27% + 11½% = 38½%, or rounded, 39%), one is able to produce a sample outcome that is consistent with the actual primary outcome.

Unfortunately, finding the correction factor and adjusting Humphrey's and McGovern's statewide percentage is only the first step in the process of correcting the sample for the bandwagon effect. Since the amount of preferential unrepresentativeness is partly dependent upon the strength of the relationship between candidate preference and socioeconomic characteristics, and since redistributing thirty-nine votes would alter that strength, some assumptions must be made about the socioeconomic identity of those thirty-nine voters. For instance, suppose we assume that the bandwagon effect centered exclusively among lower-SES elements within the party, and that, as a result, thirty-nine lower-SES Democrats switched their votes from Humphrey to McGovern in the post-election survey. By taking thirty-nine lower-SES votes away from McGovern, and by giving thirty-nine lower-SES votes to Humphrey, we would be strengthening the relationship between candidate preference and SES, and thereby increasing the amount of preferential unrepresentativeness in the primary electorate. If, on the other hand, we made the opposite assumption (that it was thirty-nine upper-SES Democrats that switched allegiance in the post-election survey), and we subtracted thirty-nine upper-SES votes from McGovern and added them to Humphrey, we would be weakening that relationship, and therefore, decreasing the amount of preferential distortion in the electorate. Thus, assumptions as to what kinds of Democrats jumped on the bandwagon are crucial.

Fortunately, one assumption does not have to be chosen and defended over another. Preferential unrepresentativeness can be computed using as many different assumptions about the source of the bandwagon effect as one is willing to make. For the purposes of this study, I have limited the number to three:

(1) that a *perfect negative* relationship exists between the bandwagon effect and socioeconomic status.
(2) that a *moderate negative* relationship exists between the bandwagon effect and socioeconomic status.
(3) that *no* relationship exists between the bandwagon effect and socioeconomic status.

Each of these assumptions was chosen for a different reason, and therefore each merits individual attention.

ASSUMPTION NUMBER ONE

The first step in computing the amount of preferential unrepresentativeness under assumption number one lies in assuming a perfect, negative relationship between the bandwagon effect and SES.[3] In other words, it will be assumed that all thirty-nine jumpers were lower-SES Democrats. The variable education will be used as the measure of socioeconomic standing: the categories eighth and under, ninth-to-eleventh, and high school will be designated as lower SES and the categories 1-3 college, college degree, and advanced college degree will be designated as upper SES. Thus, Humphrey will gain thirteen votes in each of the three lowest educational categories, and McGovern will lose thirteen votes in each of those same three categories. The three highest educational categories will remain untouched. The advantage in using this assumption is that by strengthening the relationship between candidate preference and SES to its *maximum* possible state, we will be establishing an upper limit or ceiling on the amount of preferential unrepresentativeness that did occur. Incorporation of this assumption into the second step of our calculations is illustrated in table 16.

ASSUMPTION NUMBER TWO

Based on past research on political behavior, the second assumption is probably the most reasonable. Here we assume that the relationship between the bandwagon effect and socioeconomic status is both moderate and negative, that is, that most switchers were lower-SES Democrats, but that a few were also upper-SES Democrats. A two-to-one ratio will be used to embody this relationship. Of the jumpers 67 percent (26) will come from the three lowest educational categories and 33 percent (13) will come from the three highest categories. Table 17 shows how this second assumption would modify the calculation of step two.

ASSUMPTION NUMBER THREE

In the third calculation of preferential unrepresentativeness we will assume that there was no relationship between the bandwagon effect and socioeconomic status; that is, that the bandwagon drew from all educational categories in equal proportion.[4] This possibility, although plausible, is remote since there are few types of political behavior that are not related to levels of formal education. The advantage to using it, however, lies in the fact that by depressing the relationship between SES and candidate preference to its weakest possible state, we are establishing a *minimum* or floor to the amount of preferential unrepresentativeness that did occur. Incorporation of this assumption into our calculation is illustrated in table 18.

Table 16
Step Two Under Assumption Number One

	CORRECTED n PER CATEGORY		CORRECTED CANDIDATE VOTE PER CATEGORY	CORRECTED n PER CANDIDATE
8th & under	(34)	×	$\left(\dfrac{n + 13}{N}\right)$ =	(Corrected n for Humphrey)
	(34)	×	$\left(\dfrac{n - 13}{N}\right)$ =	(Corrected n for McGovern)
9th–11th	(44)	×	$\left(\dfrac{n + 13}{N}\right)$ =	(Corrected n for Humphrey)
	(44)	×	$\left(\dfrac{n - 13}{N}\right)$ =	(Corrected n for McGovern)
High school	(105)	×	$\left(\dfrac{n + 13}{N}\right)$ =	(Corrected n for Humphrey)
	(105)	×	$\left(\dfrac{n - 13}{N}\right)$ =	(Corrected n for McGovern)
1–3 college	(99)	×	$\left(\dfrac{n}{N} \text{ or } \% \text{ for Humphrey}\right)$ =	(n for Humphrey)
	(99)	×	$\left(\dfrac{n}{N} \text{ or } \% \text{ for McGovern}\right)$ =	(n for McGovern)
Col degree	(31)	×	$\left(\dfrac{n}{N} \text{ or } \% \text{ for Humphrey}\right)$ =	(n for Humphrey)
	(31)	×	$\left(\dfrac{n}{N} \text{ or } \% \text{ for McGovern}\right)$ =	(n for McGovern)
Adv col deg	(27)	×	$\left(\dfrac{n}{N} \text{ or } \% \text{ for Humphrey}\right)$ =	(n for Humphrey)
	(27)	×	$\left(\dfrac{n}{N} \text{ or } \% \text{ for McGovern}\right)$ =	(n for McGovern)

SOURCE: California Poll 7204, Field Research Corporation, San Francisco, Calif.
NOTES: Where n = candidate's actual number of votes per subgroup
  N = total number of subgroup voters
  $\dfrac{n}{N}$ = candidate's actual percentage of subgroup vote

Table 17
Step Two Under Assumption Number Two

	CORRECTED n PER CATEGORY		CORRECTED CANDIDATE VOTE PER CATEGORY		CORRECTED n PER CANDIDATE
8th & under	(34)	×	$\left(\dfrac{n + 10}{N}\right)$	=	(Corrected n for Humphrey)
	(34)	×	$\left(\dfrac{n - 10}{N}\right)$	=	(Corrected n for McGovern)
9th–11th	(44)	×	$\left(\dfrac{n + 9}{N}\right)$	=	(Corrected n for Humphrey)
	(44)	×	$\left(\dfrac{n - 9}{N}\right)$	=	(Corrected n for McGovern)
High school	(105)	×	$\left(\dfrac{n + 7}{N}\right)$	=	(Corrected n for Humphrey)
	(105)	×	$\left(\dfrac{n - 7}{N}\right)$	=	(Corrected n for McGovern)
1-3 college	(99)	×	$\left(\dfrac{n + 6}{N}\right)$	=	(Corrected n for Humphrey)
	(99)	×	$\left(\dfrac{n - 6}{N}\right)$	=	(Corrected n for McGovern)
Col degree	(31)	×	$\left(\dfrac{n + 5}{N}\right)$	=	(Corrected n for Humphrey)
	(31)	×	$\left(\dfrac{n - 5}{N}\right)$	=	(Corrected n for McGovern)
Adv col deg	(27)	×	$\left(\dfrac{n + 2}{N}\right)$	=	(Corrected n for Humphrey)
	(27)	×	$\left(\dfrac{n - 2}{N}\right)$	=	(Corrected n for McGovern)

SOURCE: California Poll 7204, Field Research Corporation, San Francisco, Calif.
NOTES: Where n = candidate's actual number of votes per subgroup
N = total number of subgroup voters
$\dfrac{n}{N}$ = candidate's actual percentage of subgroup vote

Table 18
Step Two Under Assumption Number Three

	CORRECTED n PER CATEGORY	CORRECTED CANDIDATE VOTE PER CATEGORY	CORRECTED n PER CANDIDATE
8th & under	(34) ×	$\left(\dfrac{n+4}{N} \right)$ =	(Corrected n for Humphrey)
	(34) ×	$\left(\dfrac{n-4}{N} \right)$ =	(Corrected n for McGovern)
9th–11th	(44) ×	$\left(\dfrac{n+4}{N} \right)$ =	(Corrected n for Humphrey)
	(44) ×	$\left(\dfrac{n-4}{N} \right)$ =	(Corrected n for McGovern)
High school	(105) ×	$\left(\dfrac{n+11}{N} \right)$ =	(Corrected n for Humphrey)
	(105) ×	$\left(\dfrac{n-11}{N} \right)$ =	(Corrected n for McGovern)
1–3 college	(99) ×	$\left(\dfrac{n+12}{N} \right)$ =	(Corrected n for Humphrey)
	(99) ×	$\left(\dfrac{n-12}{N} \right)$ =	(Corrected n for McGovern)
Col degree	(31) ×	$\left(\dfrac{n+5}{N} \right)$ =	(Corrected n for Humphrey)
	(31) ×	$\left(\dfrac{n-5}{N} \right)$ =	(Corrected n for McGovern)
Adv col deg	(27) ×	$\left(\dfrac{n+5}{N} \right)$ =	(Corrected n for Humphrey)
	(27) ×	$\left(\dfrac{n-5}{N} \right)$ =	(Corrected n for McGovern)

SOURCE: California Poll 7204, Field Research Corporation, San Francisco, Calif.
NOTES: Where n = candidate's actual number of votes per subgroup
　　　　N = total number of subgroup voters
　　　　$\dfrac{n}{N}$ = candidate's actual percentage of subgroup vote

In short, the amount of preferential unrepresentativeness will be computed using the three most reasonable assumptions about the origin of the bandwagon effect. The three separate calculations will yield three different election outcomes. These three outcomes will cover the complete range of outcomes that could have occurred had the California

Democratic primary electorate been demographically representative of the California Democratic party membership. The findings are presented in table 19.

The conclusion to be drawn from table 19 is unmistakable. Had the 1972 California Democratic primary electorate been demographically representative of the party rank and file, Hubert Humphrey, not George McGovern, almost surely would have won the primary and captured all of California's delegates to the Democratic National Convention. Depending on the assumption about the origin of the bandwagon effect that one personally finds most tenable, Humphrey's margin of victory would have ranged from a modest but convincing 5 percentage points to a thin 1.5 percentage points. Since a ratio close to assumption number two, (that is, a little more or a little less than 2:1) is probably the most reasonable measure of the source of the bandwagon, Humphrey would have beaten McGovern by two to three percentage points.

Undoubtedly, had Hubert Humphrey won the California primary, he would have been the presidential nominee in 1972. It may be that any Democrat would have lost to Richard Nixon that year and, if the party had to experiment with a liberal ideologue, 1972 was a year in which the lesson learned incurred very little cost. But, then again, it is just possible that Humphrey might have won. Unfortunately, an unrepresentative primary electorate precluded the nation from ever knowing.

The 1968 California primary seems to possess less intrinsic historical importance. The candidate disadvantaged by an unrepresentative primary electorate (Robert Kennedy) still managed to beat the candidate advantaged by the bias (Eugene McCarthy). This does not detract in any way from the general finding of an inherent bias in the primary system, but it does illustrate the point that the bias can be overcome, and that it may have no significant impact on the election outcome.

In the context of the quest for the Democratic nomination in 1972, the California primary and the effect of unrepresentativeness on that out-

Table 19
California Democratic Presidential Primary Corrected for
Unrepresentativeness, 1972

	MCGOVERN	HUMPHREY
Official Primary Results	43.5%	38.6%
Primary Results Under Assumption #1	38.4%	43.4%
Primary Results Under Assumption #2	39.6%	42.2%
Primary Results Under Assumption #3	40.1%	41.6%

Source: California Poll 7204, Field Research Corporation, San Francisco, Calif.

come cannot be ignored. But to what extent are these findings unique to California? Do they apply in other states, in other years, and at other electoral levels? It is to these questions we now turn.

NOTES

1. The definition of preferential unrepresentativeness is identical to demographic unrepresentativeness: the degree of likeness between the distribution of candidate preferences within the primary electorate and its corresponding distribution within the party membership.

2. The amount of preferential unrepresentativeness is dependent upon the strength of the relationships between candidate preference and socioeconomic status and between turnout and socioeconomic status. Correcting the sample for the bandwagon effect does not in any way alter the latter relationship.

3. The relationship can be considered perfect and negative when SES is treated as a dichotomous variable.

4. Due to rounding, the number of jumpers in table 18 equals 41. The number of jumpers in each educational category was computed as follows:

	% OF PRIMARY ELECTORATE		CORRECTION FACTOR		NUMBER OF JUMPERS	% OF TOTAL
8th & under	9%	×	39	=	4	(12.9)
9th–11th grade	9%	×	39	=	4	(12.5)
High school	28%	×	39	=	11	(11.4)
1–3 college	30%	×	39	=	12	(11.6)
College degree	12%	×	39	=	5	(12.8)
Advanced col deg	12%	×	39	=	5	(12.8)

SOURCE: California Poll 7204, Field Research Corporation, San Francisco, Calif.

Notice that the percentage of jumpers from each educational category is nearly identical.

5

UNREPRESENTATIVENESS IN OTHER PRESIDENTIAL PRIMARIES

THE PRIMARY inquiry, so far, has been restricted to a specific set of questions about California, and for California the findings are conclusive. But is California's experience with primaries unique or typical? Does demographic unrepresentativeness exist in other states and in primaries at other electoral levels? Are issues, ideology, and candidate preferences similarly related to the socioeconomic status of Democrats in other states? Answers to these questions are crucial because they determine to some extent the ramifications of unrepresentativeness for the Democratic party. A permanent bias advantaging the upper social and economic strata within the party, from the local to the national level, in primary after primary, year after year, might produce substantial shifts in the content and direction of party policy, and hence, in the party's constituent base. On the other hand, random unrepresentativeness either within a specific campaign (that is, under-representation of lower-SES Democrats in some states and upper-SES Democrats in others), or across several campaigns (over-representation of upper-SES Democrats one year, under-representation the next), might have no measurable long-term impact. The use of principles of electoral behavior and an analysis of data from four other 1972 presidential primaries, may shed some light on these crucial questions.

As noted in chapter 2, demographic unrepresentativeness in Democratic primaries is a function of particular patterns of partisanship and turnout within the population. The extent to which the patterns in California are mirrored elsewhere determines the extent to which demographic unrepresentativeness plagues the nomination process of the Democratic party nationwide. There is sufficient reason to believe that demographic unrepresentativeness is not solely confined to one state (California), or to one type of primary (presidential), but that its presence and particular direction exist in other states and in primaries for most electoral offices contested by Democrats.

In the first place, the pattern of party cleavage within California is probably more typical than atypical of party cleavage nationwide and within most large, urban, and industrialized states. Democratic party identification both in California and nationwide tends to be disproportionately but not exclusively lower-SES (socioeconomic status), that is, composed of racial and religious minorities, blue-collar workers, the poor, and the less-educated.[1] The congruity between California and the nation at large is not surprising for a number of reasons. First, California has a diverse social and economic base. It has a heterogeneous population. It has extensive urban, suburban, and rural areas. It has commerce, industry, and agriculture. It has pockets of liberalism, radicalism, and sunbelt conservatism. In short, it has nearly everything the nation has, but in smaller doses and varying degrees. Second, historical forces, such as the depression and New Deal, and social forces, such as the socialization process, which combine to shape the partisan identification of the electorate, do not honor state boundaries. They are constants and, as such, influence and reinforce partisanship regardless of geographical setting.

Admittedly, local and regional factors also shape partisan attachment, and for this reason differences do exist between states. But the same social, economic, and political diversity that accounts for the similarity between California and the nation also accounts for the similarity between California and most large, urban, industrialized states. Given marginal changes in the strength of the relationships, figure 2 could pass for Democratic partisanship in most of the ten most populous states. And at last count, all ten held presidential primaries.[2] In addition, these ten states supply a majority of delegates to the Democratic National Convention.

The second condition necessary for demographic unrepresentativeness to appear in other states is a relationship between SES and primary turnout similar to that found in California. In both California primaries turnout was strongly related to socioeconomic status. Upper-SES Democrats outvoted their lower-SES counterparts by as much as 40 to 50 percentage points. This relationship between status and turnout is not unique to California nor to presidential primaries. After thirty years of empirical research on these matters, there have been few studies to date which have not found most forms of political participation to be socioeconomically related. While it is true that the strength of the relationship varies depending on the type of election (that is, midterm vs. presidential, primary vs. general), on the level of electoral competition (statewide office vs. national office), and on the mode of participation (voting vs. contributing vs. attending political meetings), the direction of the relationship has reached the state of an immutable "law."

Given these two constants, one would be hard pressed to argue the uniqueness of either the presence or direction of demographic unrepresentativeness in the state of California. One is on less firm ground, however, when speaking about magnitude, for it does vary from state to state, year to year, and electoral office to electoral office. Eventually, additional studies in other states and in other types of primaries will confirm these differences. But for now, and in the absence of such studies, one need not resort to a crystal ball. Reasonable inferences about the magnitude of demographic unrepresentativeness in other states can be drawn from two other variables: the size of the state's turnout in relationship to California's, and the presence or absence of intermediary organizations.

First, turnout in California's Democratic presidential primaries is significantly higher than in any other state. As indicated by figure 3, 66 percent of all California Democrats voted in 1972, and 64 percent voted in 1968. Turnout in other states ranged from 10 percentage points to 50 percentage points lower. Pennsylvania, for example, had a turnout of 49 percent in 1972 and 33 percent in 1968. New York's, Oregon's, and Rhode Island's were even lower.

The trend continued into 1976. Table 20 presents Democratic primary turnout for every state holding a closed primary in 1976.[3] Turnout is computed by dividing the number of votes cast by the number of registered Democrats.

Table 20
Turnout in Closed Democratic
Presidential Primaries—1976

California	72%
Oregon	61%
Nevada	60%
Massachusetts	57%
Florida	55%
New Hampshire	53%
West Virginia	53%
Nebraska	51%
Pennsylvania	49%
Maryland	48%
North Carolina	35%
South Dakota	33%
Kentucky	28%

SOURCE: Austin Ranney, *Participation in American Presidential Elections 1976* (Washington, D.C.: American Enterprise Institute, 1977), p. 23.

In keeping with its tradition, California again topped the turnout list with 72 percent of its registered Democrats going to the polls. Compared with turnout in other states, California's figure ranged from 11 percentage points (Oregon) higher to 44 percentage points (Kentucky) higher. The average for the thirteen states was 50 percent. California's turnout exceeded this mean by 22 percentage points.

This marked difference between California and other states is crucial to the analysis of magnitude because of a second interrelated factor, socioeconomic drop-off. As primary turnout reaches 100 percent, the party membership equals the primary electorate and perfect representation is achieved. But as turnout decreases, it decreases unevenly among subpopulations. Lower-SES Democrats drop out of the electorate in larger proportions than upper-SES Democrats. In other words, holding all other variables constant, a percentage drop in overall turnout is accounted for by a larger number of lower-SES Democrats than upper-SES Democrats. Because of this socioeconomic related attrition, each percentage difference in turnout between California and other states probably denotes *even greater degrees of demographic unrepresentativeness* elsewhere. That is, as a group, the better-educated, higher-income, and upper-class Democrats are likely to be more over-represented in those states whose turnouts are lower than California's. On the other hand, less-educated, lower-income, and lower-class Democrats are likely to be more under-represented.

The inverse of this argument receives a great deal of attention during general elections. Incremental increases in turnout, the argument goes, are accounted for by a greater influx of lower-SES voters into the electorate than upper-SES voters. Lower-SES individuals tend to be disproportionately Democratic in party affiliation; upper-SES, disproportionately Republican. Assuming, of course, that party identification plays a decisive role in candidate choice, a Democratic candidate should benefit from any incremental increase in turnout.

One must be careful, however, when generalizing about the magnitude of demographic unrepresentativeness based solely on turnout. The linkage is contingent upon all other things being equal and, in the real world of politics, this is rarely the case. Factors do vary from state to state and from year to year which could alter the amount of socioeconomic drop-off regardless of overall turnout. Strong intermediary organizations, such as state or local parties, or labor unions, are examples of this type of intervening variable. Because of their mobilizing ability among lower-SES Democrats, their presence in one state and their absence in another may mean lower-SES participation in the former than in the latter. Hence, a state with these organizations will probably suffer less demographic unrepresentativeness than a state without them.

Viewed together, size of turnout and the presence of intermediary organizations could be used to roughly group and rank states according to the degree of unrepresentativeness one might find in their presidential primaries. The first group—the large- and medium-sized states with low turnout and with few or weak mediating organizations—probably experiences the greatest degree of unrepresentativeness. Democratic presidential primaries held in the south and in states such as Oregon, Massachusetts, and Wisconsin probably fall into this category.

Ranked second in degree of unrepresentativeness are those states with low turnouts but with many or strong intermediary organizations. Most of the large, competitive two-party states meet these conditions. Included in this group are states such as Illinois, Indiana, Michigan, New Jersey, Ohio, and Pennsylvania. Recently, however, the influence of mediating organizations has begun to wane. Few strong statewide Democratic party organizations exist. Few local party organizations mobilize their adherents for presidential primaries, especially if state and local primaries are held on different days. The ability of labor unions has always been suspect, and their track record in 1972 and 1976 removes little of that doubt. Ironically, it has been primaries that have weakened these organizations, but it is also these organizations, when healthy and active, that bring some degree of representativeness to the primary system.

The third tier includes those states with high turnout and few or weak mediating organizations. It is into this category that California falls. The most representative primaries would be found in states with high turnouts and strong intermediary organizations. Unfortunately for the Democratic party few, if any, states presently conducting presidential primaries meet these two conditions.

Based on the preceding analysis, it does not seem unreasonable to infer that California provides a particularly strong test case. If unrepresentativeness exists on this scale in a state where indications point to the problem being minimal at worst, then logic can only lead to the conclusion that the magnitude of demographic unrepresentativeness in other states is, at least, equal to but more likely greater than that found in California. Trends toward both lower turnouts (see chapter 2) and weaker intermediary organizations suggest the possibility of even greater degrees of demographic unrepresentativeness in presidential primary electorates of the future.

With some caution, the same reasoning can be applied to Democratic primaries at the state and local level. Since turnout is less in state and local elections, the magnitude of unrepresentativeness in these primaries may be greater. One should remember, however, that as districts (and states) become smaller, turnout plays a less-important role, since party membership becomes more homogeneous. As noted in chapter 2, class-based (or homogeneous) parties are immune to demographic unrepresentativeness.

Although the presence, direction, and magnitude of demographic unrepresentativeness in other states can be inferred from certain basic principles of voting behavior, the *political* significance of this finding must be held in abeyance until we can also confirm the presence of an additional relationship, a relationship between candidate preference and SES similar to that found in California. The continual under-representation of black Democrats, or blue-collar Democrats, or less-educated Democrats has no effect whatsoever on the political fate of particular candidates or issues if these under-represented groups do not gravitate toward certain types of candidates, or if their allegiance arbitrarily shifts from state to state. In either case, the presence of a systematic demographic bias fails to produce a systematic preferential bias since the advantages and disadvantages are either offset or randomly distributed during the course of the campaign.

The presence or absence in states other than California of a relationship between candidate preferences and SES can be tested by reference to survey data collected in four other presidential primaries in 1972. The states to be examined are Wisconsin, Florida, Michigan, and Pennsylvania. The surveys were commissioned by the *New York Times* and *Time* and were conducted by the polling firm of Yankelovich, Skelly, and White, Inc.[4]

The advantages of these data are self-evident. First, all four primaries were contested by major contenders, and each contender managed to win at least one of these primaries. Humphrey won in Pennsylvania, McGovern won in Wisconsin, and Wallace won in Florida and Michigan. Thus, by narrowing the field to three factional leaders, these early primaries set the stage for the critical showdown in California. Second, the surveys contain some variables that will allow us to trace candidate preferences across states and time and to determine whether they were also linked, as they were in California, to the socioeconomic status of Democrats. Third, because the data were collected by a single polling organization asking identical questions and using identical sampling techniques, interstate comparisons of these relationships are possible.

Naturally, since the surveys were designed to measure only broad, general voting patterns, some drawbacks to the data also exist. First, as Appendix 3 shows, the number of demographic variables differed from state to state and only a few of those variables tapped the respondent's socioeconomic status. The variables "education" and "income," two excellent indicators of socioeconomic status, were each used only in one state. On the other hand, occupation and race, two adequate but less reliable indicators, were used in three and four states, respectively. Second, the range of internal variation within each variable was small. For example, the variable "income" consisted of two categories, "under $10,000" and "over $10,000." The variable "education" consisted of three categories: "less than high school," "high school," and "some college or more." As a result a good deal of precision was lost.

The first presidential primary in 1972 was held in the state of New Hampshire. Going into the nation's first primary, Senator Edmund Muskie was the front-runner, and it looked to all observers as if the nomination was his for the asking. But in New Hampshire, South Dakota's Senator, George McGovern, finished second with a surprising 37 percent of the vote and this unexpected showing earned him top billing in newspaper headlines. The scorecard after one primary read McGovern 1, Muskie 0.

The nation's attention next shifted to Florida. Here for the first time, all major contenders were on one ballot. The state was generally conceded to be Wallace country, so eleven candidates vied for the runner-up position. Wallace did indeed win with 42 percent of the vote. The "place" and "show" money went to Humphrey and Jackson with 19 percent and 14 percent respectively. Edmund Muskie finished a distant fourth with only 10 percent of the vote, and George McGovern finished sixth with 6 percent of the vote.

Florida's presidential primary in 1972 was closed and therefore restricted to registered Democrats. If one assumes the presence of socioeconomic-related turnout, and there is no reason to believe otherwise, one can infer the presence of preferential unrepresentativeness by uncovering socioeconomic-related candidate preferences.[5] The candidate preferences of lower-SES Democrats will be under-represented in primary electorates due to the under-representation of those subgroups. For candidate preferences of upper-SES Democrats the reverse is true. Table 21 cross-tabulates candidate choice in the 1972 Florida primary by the educational level of its Democratic voters.

As early as this second primary in the nation in 1972, and even among a field of eleven candidates, the constituent support of the major contenders was already beginning to form and divide along the same socioeconomic lines that polarized the California electorate three months and thirteen primaries later. Hubert Humphrey's support in Florida, just as in California, rested with Democrats with less than a high school education. He received 31 percent of their vote, which was 13 percentage points higher than his statewide average and 19 percentage points higher than his support among better-educated Democrats. These are the same types of individuals whose partisanship is overwhelmingly Democratic, whose ideological self-identification bends toward the

Table 21
Candidate Choice by Education—Florida, 1972

	LESS THAN HIGH SCHOOL	HIGH SCHOOL	SOME COLLEGE OR MORE
Wallace	47%	45%	31%
Humphrey	31%	15%	12%
Jackson	3%	16%	19%
Muskie	11%	7%	10%
McGovern	2%	2%	13%
Others[a]	6%	15%	15%
	100%	100%	100%
n =	105	148	134

SOURCE: Recomputed from 1972 *New York Times/Time/*Yankelovich, Skelly, and White, Inc. Primary Surveys
[a] McCarthy, Lindsay, Chisholm, Mills, Yorty, Hartke voters

moderate to conservative end of the continuum, whose support the party needs for electoral victory in November, but whose turnout rate contributes to their own under-representation, and to the under-representation of their candidates in primary electorates.[6]

George McGovern, on the other hand, was already attracting the support of Democrats at the other end of the SES continuum. His support among better-educated Democrats (13%) was six and one-half times greater than his support among less educated (2%) and moderately educated Democrats (2%). In fact, his appeal among better-educated Democrats, who tend to be a minority within the party, but who also tend to turn out in much larger proportions in primaries, was directly responsible for what the press labeled a "respectable" 6 percent of the vote and sixth-place finish.

Senator Henry Jackson's support among better-educated Democrats was also six times greater than his support among less-educated Democrats. But over-representation of Jackson sentiment in the primary electorate, and the over-representation of candidates like Jackson, presents much less of a problem to the Democratic party. In the Florida primary, Jackson's support among better-educated Democrats was largely a reflection of his support among the state's large Jewish population. Jews, as a group, tend to be better-educated. Jews also gave Jackson the largest percentage of their vote. But Jews also tend to be overwhelmingly Democratic as well. Thus Jackson's over-representation actually connotes an over-representation of a traditional Democratic group whose support is vital to the Democratic party in the general election. As noted in chapter 2, the Democratic party can probably live with, and win with, this type of over-representation in its nomination process.

The vote for George Wallace in Florida was also socioeconomically related. His largest percentage came from Democrats with less than a high school education (47%), and his smallest percentage came from Democrats with some college experience or more (31%). Thus, at first glance, one might argue that the Florida outcome may have, to some extent, under-represented Wallace sentiment within the state. On the other hand, one must also recognize the regional nature of the contest. Wallace could expect to and did, in fact, receive far more support from all three educational subgroups than any other candidate in the race. Thus, an under-representation of his less-educated followers was offset by an over-representation of his better-educated followers.

Race, like education, can also be used to infer preferential unrepresentativeness since it also is related to turnout. Candidates with overwhelming support among black Democrats will be under-represented in primary electorates since blacks as a group are under-represented. Conversely, white Democrats, and the candidates they support, will be over-represented. Fortunately, the variable race was used in all four states. Table 22 cross-tabulates candidate choice by race in Florida, Pennsylvania, Wisconsin, and Michigan.

In all four states, Hubert Humphrey was the overwhelming choice of black Democrats. His percentage of the black vote ranged from 55 percent and 56 percent in Florida and Michigan, to 73 percent and 75 percent in Wisconsin and Pennsylvania. Thus, he was again the only candidate whose final vote tally in all four states suffered from the unrepresentative nature of their primary electorates.

George McGovern and George Wallace, on the other hand, would have lost votes in all four states if the primary electorates had been racially representative of the party rank and file. McGovern's percentage of the black vote ranged from 1 percent in Florida to 25 percent in Michigan. In all four states McGovern's support among white Democrats exceeded his support among black Democrats and in three of the four states the margin approximated 2:1 or worse. George Wallace's vote in all four states was drawn almost exclusively from white Democrats.

Two different occupation variables were used in Wisconsin, Pennsylvania, and Michigan. The first categorized respondents by the occupation of the head-of-household. The second divided the sample according to the respondent's occupation. Although both variables consisted of a small number of categories, they are still useful since they both include the white-collar/blue-collar distinction which was found in California to be related to both turnout and candidate choice.[7]

Table 23 cross-tabulates candidate choice in Wisconsin, Pennsylvania,

Table 22
Candidate Choice by Race—1972

	FLORIDA		PENNSYLVANIA		WISCONSIN		MICHIGAN	
	White	*Black*	*White*	*Black*	*White*	*Black*	*White*	*Black*
Humphrey	11%	55%	29%	75%	19%	73%	11%	56%
McGovern	7%	1%	22%	9%	32%	17%	27%	25%
Wallace	49%	2%	23%	9%	22%	—	57%	6%
Muskie	10%	7%	22%	7%	11%	10%	2%	1%
Jackson	16%	2%	4%	—	8%	—	—	—
Lindsay	5%	19%	—	—	7%	—	—	—
Chisholm	2%	15%	—	—	1%	—	—	—
Others[a]	—	—	—	—	—	—	3%	13%
	100%	101%[b]	100%	100%	100%	100%	100%	101%[b]
n =	324	64	375	35	363	19	366	42

SOURCE: Recomputed from 1972 *New York Times/Time*/Yankelovich, Skelly, and White, Inc. Primary Surveys

[a] McCarthy, Mills, Yorty, and Hartke voters in Florida. Jackson, Lindsay, and Chisholm were combined into "Other" category in Michigan.

[b] Due to rounding.

Table 23

Candidate Choice by Occupation of Head-of-Household—1972

	WISCONSIN				PENNSYLVANIA			MICHIGAN		
	White-Collar	Blue-Collar	Farmer	Other	White-Collar	Blue-Collar	Other	White-Collar	Blue-Collar	Other
Humphrey	16%	28%	17%	19%	23%	36%	54%	12%	16%	29%
McGovern	35%	25%	32%	41%	26%	17%	14%	34%	22%	25%
Wallace	15%	26%	31%	8%	22%	25%	11%	46%	58%	40%
Muskie	9%	12%	7%	17%	22%	20%	21%	2%	2%	3%
Lindsay	12%	2%	8%	—	4%	—	—	—	—	—
Jackson	11%	5%	3%	15%	2%	2%	—	—	—	—
Other	2%	2%	2%	—	—	1%	—	6%	2%	3%
	100%	100%	100%	100%	99%ᵃ	101%ᵃ	100%	100%	100%	100%
n =	146	165	42	29	186	170	58	152	214	44

SOURCE: Recomputed from 1972 *New York Times/Time/*Yankelovich, Skelly, and White, Inc. Primary Surveys

ᵃDue to rounding.

and Michigan by the occupation of the head-of-household. In both Wisconsin and Pennsylvania, just as in California, Hubert Humphrey received the largest percentage of the blue-collar vote, capturing 28 percent in Wisconsin and 36 percent in Pennsylvania. In contrast, his percentage of the white-collar vote in both states was 12 to 13 percentage points lower.

George McGovern, on the other hand, was preferred by white-collar Democrats in both states, receiving 35 percent of their vote in Wisconsin and 26 percent of their vote in Pennsylvania. His support from this group exceeded his support from blue-collar Democrats by 9 to 10 percentage points.

In Michigan, both Humphrey and McGovern fell to George Wallace and the busing issue. But in spite of a Wallace romp, in which the Alabama governor captured a huge percentage of both white-collar and blue-collar voters, Humphrey's and McGovern's base of support still remained somewhat intact.

Table 24 cross-tabulates candidate choice in all three states by occupation of respondent. Since only two extra occupations (housewives and farmers) are differentiated within this variable, the pattern of candidate choice varies little from the pattern uncovered using the occupation of the head-of-household. Humphrey's support is derived from blue-collar Democrats. McGovern's support is derived from white-collar Democrats. Wallace's support, when strong, is derived from both.

The only other socioeconomic variable used in the 1972 survey was income. It was used only in Michigan, and it consisted of two categories: "under $10,000," and "over $10,000." Despite its poor design, the variable is still useful. Income, like education, race, and occupation is related to primary turnout. If candidate choices are similarly related, preferential unrepresentativeness results. Table 25 cross-tabulates candidate choice in Michigan by income and the findings are mixed.

Humphrey's source of support among income subgroups is consistent with his source of support among occupational and racial subgroups. He captured the votes of nearly one out of every four lower-income Democrats, but lost the votes of nine out of ten upper-income Democrats.

McGovern, on the other hand, derived nearly equal amounts of support from both income categories, and Wallace was the overwhelming favorite of both.

Because of the small number of socioeconomic indicators used in these four surveys, and because of the limited internal variation within each indicator, findings based on these data alone are hardly definitive. Yet these findings in fact parallel the more comprehensive ones from California. When both sets of findings are viewed together they lend

Table 24
Candidate Choice by Occupation of Respondent—1972

	WISCONSIN					PENNSYLVANIA					MICHIGAN				
	White-Collar	Blue-Collar	Housewife	Farmer	Other	White-Collar	Blue-Collar	Housewife	Farmer	Other	White-Collar	Blue-Collar	Housewife	Farmer	Other
Humphrey	19%	29%	19%	17%	19%	25%	34%	35%	100%	40%	13%	17%	16%	—	17%
McGovern	31%	24%	29%	22%	52%	24%	13%	21%	—	24%	32%	18%	22%	—	49%
Wallace	17%	30%	14%	43%	10%	24%	29%	18%	—	15%	47%	62%	55%	100%	27%
Muskie	10%	11%	17%	4%	6%	19%	22%	23%	—	22%	2%	2%	4%	—	—
Jackson	12%	4%	9%	4%	4%	6%	2%	2%	—	—	—	—	—	—	—
Lindsay	9%	2%	10%	6%	6%	—	—	—	—	—	—	1%	—	—	—
Others	2%	1%	1%	4%	2%	3%	1%	—	—	—	6%		4%	—	7%
	100%	101%[a]	99%[a]	100%	99%[a]	101%[a]	101%[a]	99%[a]	100%	101%[a]	100%	100%	101%[a]	100%	100%
n =	115	108	83	25	50	128	95	123	2	66	109	131	112	1	56

SOURCE: Recomputed from 1972 *New York Times/Time*/Yankelovich, Skelly, and White, Inc. Primary Surveys
[a] Due to rounding.

Table 25
Candidate Choice by Income—
Michigan—1972

	UNDER $10,000	OVER $10,000
Humphrey	23%	10%
McGovern	27%	28%
Wallace	42%	58%
Muskie	2%	2%
Other	7%	2%
	101%[a]	100%
n =	179	226

SOURCE: Recomputed from 1972 *New York Times/Time/*Yankelovich, Skelly, and White, Inc. Primary Surveys
[a] Due to rounding.

themselves to certain generalizations about a nomination system based almost exclusively on presidential primaries: it bestows advantages and disadvantages upon certain recognizable types of candidates, issues, and constituents within the Democratic party.

Since 1968 the Democratic party at the elite level has been split into three discernible factions. The three camps are usually designated New Deal, Reform/Activist (or New Politics), and Southern. Each can be distinguished by its own set of national spokesmen; its own set of positions on major social, economic, and foreign policy issues; and its own set of constituents within the party rank and file. The New Deal faction, a product of the political and economic philosophy of the Roosevelt era, is marked by its liberal position on most economic issues, its moderate-to-conservative position on most social issues, and its interventionist position on foreign policy. Rank-and-file support for the New Deal faction, its candidates, and its issue-concerns tends to be less-educated, lower-income, urban, blue-collar, and non-Southern. The New Politics faction, dissatisfied with the social and foreign policy of the New Deal leadership of the late 1960s, split from those ranks and emerged as an alternative voice within the party by taking a more permissive social stance and a more isolationist foreign policy position. Rank-and-file support tends to be upper-SES, white-collar, and suburban. The Southern wing, a remnant of the Civil War, completes the troika. This faction tends to be much more conservative on economic and social questions, and much more aggressive on foreign policy matters. Rank-and-file support tends to be regional, but it can transcend region when a sufficiently controversial social issue appears. These three factions and their respective issue positions and constituents are outlined in Figure 11.

As figure 11 shows, the New Deal faction acts both as a bond and buffer between the New Politics and Southern wings. It acts as a bond since it shares similar issue positions with each. The New Deal and New Politics faction agree on economic policy. The New Deal and Southern factions share an affinity on most social and foreign policy matters. The New Politics and Southern factions, finally, share little in common except a label—Democrat.

Prior to the recent changes in the nomination process, the New Deal faction benefited most from any advantages that the rules of the game dispensed. In the pre-Reform era most delegates were chosen by conventions and caucuses. Old-fashioned party convention/caucus systems tended to advantage candidates with an organization, and since the New Deal faction reliably controlled party machinery in most parts of the country, it was their candidates who amassed the delegates or their delegates who controlled the convention and chose the nominee.

In today's nomination system, a system which relies heavily upon presidential primaries, the advantage has shifted. The New Politics faction, its candidates, and its issue-concerns are advantaged, since the constituency to which these kinds of candidates and issues appeal is over-represented in presidential primary electorates. This over-representation of New Politics support in primary electorates will be translated into an over-representation of delegates which, even if tied to several different New Politics candidacies, will magnify New Politics sentiment at the convention, in its credentials, rules, and platform committees, and on the floor itself.

For the New Deal faction, the reverse is true. An under-representation of its constituents in primary electorates produces an under-representation in delegates, and hence, an under-representation of its issue-concerns and candidate preferences at the convention.

Because of the regional rather than socioeconomic nature of its constituency, the Southern wing is neither directly helped nor harmed by unrepresentativeness. In the south, Southern candidates like Jimmy Carter and George Wallace can amass huge percentages of the vote across all socioeconomic levels. Thus, under-representation of their support among lower-SES southerners is offset by an over-representation of their support among upper-SES southerners. Outside the south, southern-based candidates are also adequately represented in primary electorates since their support tends to center among middle-income and moderately educated Democrats, whose turnout usually

FIGURE 11 Political Composition of Democratic Party

	ECONOMIC	SOCIAL	FOREIGN POLICY	CONSTITUENCY
New Politics	Liberal	Liberal	Isolationist	Upper SES, Suburban, White-Collar
New Deal	Liberal	Moderate	Interventionist	Lower SES, Urban, Blue-Collar
Southern	Conservative	Conservative	Interventionist	South

approximates the state mean. When viewed in conjunction with the under-representation of the New Deal faction, this full representation of the Southern faction magnifies its influence in the nomination process as well.

Although presidential primaries have held a preeminent position within the presidential nomination process since 1968, they do not constitute the total picture from which nomination outcomes can be explained. The presidential nomination process is a vast network of institutions, procedures, and rules, each of which contributes a particular bias of its own. Some of these biases are strong; others are weak. Some may reinforce the direction of bias introduced by unrepresentative primary electorates, others may reduce it. In short, the advantages and disadvantages inherent in a primary system cannot by themselves deliver victory or defeat. Robert Kennedy, for example, managed to overcome this built-in obstacle and defeat Eugene McCarthy in the 1968 California presidential primary. Morris Udall, on the other hand, could not convert this structural advantage into a Democratic nomination in 1976. This does not mean, for either man, that the bias was absent, but only that other factors (strategies, resources, ideological composition of the field, and external events) also played an important role. But if these two cases suggest the inadequacy of primary unrepresentativeness as a sole explanatory variable, it is still interesting, and probably more than coincidental, that *both* Democratic nominees in the post-Reform era were representatives of factions that *were* advantaged by the unrepresentative nature of Democratic presidential primary electorates.

Given these two related effects—the powerful influence of unrepresentativeness, but the ability of other factors to condition the political impact of that unrepresentativeness—it seems worth looking, in chapter 6, at a few other aspects of presidential primaries which have heretofore been unexplored by students of American politics.

NOTES

1. For data on national partisanship see Frank J. Sorauf, *Party Politics in America* 3d ed. (Boston: Little, Brown and Co., 1976), pp. 149–62.

2. The ten most populous states in order are: California, New York, Pennsylvania, Texas, Illinois, Ohio, Michigan, New Jersey, Florida, and Massachusetts.

3. Fourteen states and the District of Columbia held closed presidential primaries in 1976. The fourteen were California, Florida, Kentucky, Maryland, Massachusetts, Nebraska, Nevada, New Hampshire, New York, North Carolina, Oregon, Pennsylvania, South Dakota, and West Virginia. In New York and the District of Columbia registration figures were not available. Since turnout could not be computed, they were excluded from table 20.

4. Each survey contained about 38 questions. The samples consisted of ran-

domly selected cross sections of each state's Democratic primary electorate. The number of respondents ranged from 383 in Wisconsin, 388 in Florida, 410 in Michigan, to 414 in Pennsylvania. Each voter was interviewed as he left the polls thereby eliminating the possibility of a bandwagon effect. Appendix 2, which compares the official primary results to the Yankelovich/*New York Times*/*Time* survey results shows that the samples were indeed well-drawn. In each state, the candidate choices of the survey respondents are nearly identical to the candidate choices of the Democratic primary voters.

5. The strength of the relationship between socioeconomic characteristics and turnout might be weaker than expected due to the busing issue. It is unlikely however that this issue could have eliminated the relationship altogether or reversed its direction.

6. Ideological self-identification was similarly linked in Florida, as it was in California, to the educational level of Democrats. In Florida, better-educated Democrats identified themselves as moderate to liberal and less-educated Democrats identified themselves as moderate to conservative.

7. The third category in the "Occupation of Head-of-Household" was "Other." This category included students, the retired, the unemployed, farmers (in Pennsylvania and Michigan), and anyone else whose occupation did not fit into the traditional white-collar/blue-collar distinction.

6

PRESIDENTIAL PRIMARIES: FURTHER EXPLORATIONS

BEFORE THE advent of presidential primaries, state and local party organizations controlled delegate selection because most delegates were chosen in state and local party conventions and caucuses which the party organization ran. Party control of delegate selection went hand in hand with party control of candidate recruitment, and party control of both usually limited to a few the number of serious contenders seeking the party's nomination. The proliferation of presidential primaries and the switch from winner-take-all to proportional systems of delegate allocation, on the other hand, made party control much more tenuous. And, presumably, this greatly weakened party control made running for the party's highest honor as easy as throwing one's hat into an imaginary ring. The end result of these changes should have been more competitive campaigns with larger numbers and wider assortments of presidential contenders than ever before.

One way to determine whether the proliferation of presidential primaries by itself or in conjunction with other rule changes indeed produced a flood of presidential contenders is to compare the number of contenders in the post-Reform era (1972–1976) with the number of presidential hopefuls in preceding years. If presidential primaries do open up the nomination process, the number of Democratic presidential aspirants should have increased. Table 26 compares the number of Democratic contenders in three historical periods: the Roosevelt era (1932–1948), the pre-Reform era (1952–1968), and the post-Reform era (1972–1976).[1]

As table 26 shows, the number of Democratic presidential contenders increased following the rule changes.[2] In election years preceding the reforms, an average of two to four contenders vied for the party's nomination. After the reforms, the average soared to twelve, an increase of 300 percent. Not surprisingly, the lowest average (2.4) occurred during the Roosevelt era. Undoubtedly, the powers of incumbency, Roosevelt's personal popularity, and back-to-back crises (depression, World War II) discouraged all but the most intense (and foolhardy) Democrats from

Table 26
Proliferation of Democratic Presidential Contenders

	TOTAL NUMBER OF CONTENDERS	AVERAGE NUMBER PER ELECTION YEAR
Roosevelt era (1932–1948)	12	2.4
Pre-Reform era (1952–1968)	20	4.0
Post-Reform era (1972–1976)	24	12.0

Source: *Presidential Elections Since 1789* 2d ed. (Washington, D.C.: Congressional Quarterly Inc., 1979), pp. 129–73.

making the challenge. The average number of challengers during the pre-Reform era exceeded the average during the Roosevelt era, since the later period lacked the restraining influence of an incumbent in four out of the five elections.

It is possible, of course, that the dramatic increase in the number of presidential contenders in the post-Reform era is primarily a function of an open contest in both years, that is, the absence of a Democratic incumbent seeking renomination, rather than the change in the rules per se. To test this alternative explanation, table 27 controls for the absence of an incumbent by comparing the average of the post-Reform era with the average of those years in the two preceding eras in which no Democratic incumbent sought renomination. The election years prior to 1972 that lacked a Democratic incumbent were 1932, 1952, 1956, 1960, and 1968.

Table 27 eliminates the absence of an incumbent as an alternative explanation for the increase. The average during the incumbentless post-Reform era still exceeded by almost a three to one ratio the average during the incumbentless elections of the Roosevelt and pre-Reform eras. Thus, at the very least, more recent Democratic campaigns have attracted more contenders, and the data strongly suggest that this increase is in some sense a product of the reforms.

A second question of interest, and a corollary to the first, is whether the changes also increased the level of competition. One cannot assume that an increase in the number of contenders automatically raised the competitive level of the contest. The possibility exists that many of those candidates who received 1 percent of the vote in two or more primaries failed to receive 10 percent of the vote in any one primary. Thus the changes could have increased the number of contenders (since politi-

Table 27
Democratic Contenders Controlling for the Absence of Democratic Incumbents

	NUMBER OF CONTENDERS	AVERAGE PER ELECTION YEAR
Roosevelt era/pre-Reform era (1932, 1952, 1956, 1960, 1968)	21	4.2
Post-Reform era (1972, 1976)	24	12.0

SOURCE: *Presidential Elections Since 1789* 2d ed. (Washington, D.C.: Congressional Quarterly Inc., 1979), pp. 129–73.

cians might perceive the process to be more open and amenable to good luck) without necessarily increasing the competitiveness of the campaign (where openness is no guarantee of political strength).

In order to answer this question, and to show the transformation over time of primaries into nomination battlegrounds, table 28 compares the proportion of competitive presidential primaries in the three historical periods. A primary is considered competitive if at least 50,000 votes were cast and if the margin of victory between the winner and runner-up was less than 20 percentage points.[3] The findings are presented in table 28.

Table 28 shows a substantial increase over time in the percentage of

Table 28
Proliferation of Competitive Presidential Primaries

	ROOSEVELT ERA 1932–1948	PRE-REFORM ERA 1952–1968	POST-REFORM ERA 1972–1976
Competitive	9% (12)	17% (26)	40% (37)
Noncompetitive	91% (123)	83% (126)	60% (55)
	100%	100%	100%
n =	(135)	(152)	(92)

SOURCE: *Presidential Elections Since 1789* 2d ed. (Washington, D.C.: Congressional Quarterly Inc., 1979), pp. 129–73.

competitive presidential primaries. Over the last 44 years there were 379 presidential primaries, of which 20 percent were competitive. From 1932 to 1948 only 9 percent of all primaries were competitive. From 1948 to 1968 the percentage nearly doubled. But it was not until after the reforms of the late 1960s that the number of competitive primaries took a quantum jump upward.

Within limits, competition within political parties, like competition within any type of organization, is a healthy phenomenon. It forces mutual adjustment, increases organizational responsiveness, promotes internal communication, and prevents organizational atrophy. When viewed in this light, the findings in tables 26 and 28 might produce a sigh of relief in some political quarters. On the other hand, an increase in the number of primaries and in their competitive level maximizes the impact of unrepresentative primary electorates on the nomination process. Primary elections decided by 30 to 40 percentage points will still be demographically and preferentially unrepresentative, but unrepresentativeness will have little effect on delegate totals, primary outcomes, and the media exposure, money, and momentum that accompany each. But, given the increases in the number of primaries and in the number of contenders, and given the more competitive nature of primaries, unrepresentativeness looms as a much larger threat: a shift of a few percentage points can alter the entire course of a campaign, as the 1972 California primary readily illustrated.

Moreover, competitiveness within a political party can also be harmful to the party's ultimate electoral prospects, especially if competition is based on ideological differences, and if it is allowed to fester unchecked for the four-month duration of the primary season. Competitiveness in a high-stakes, zero-sum game like a presidential nomination, is only two short tempers removed from divisiveness. Divisiveness, in turn, if related to the factional structure of a party, can easily lead to open party warfare. If conflict among party elites over issues, ideology, or a candidate is allowed to spill over into the rank and file, it forces a choosing of sides at the mass level as well, and this can destroy the harmony and cooperation among the party's contributors, workers, and voters that is needed to defeat the opposition in the November election.

DIVISIVE PRESIDENTIAL PRIMARIES AND PARTY ELECTORAL PROSPECTS, 1932–1976

To what extent do presidential primaries splinter the party membership along preferential or ideological lines and what effect, if any, does this have on the party's general election prospects? Previous research on the question of whether competitive (or divisive) primaries hurt a party's chances in general elections has resulted in contradictory findings.[4] In a fifteen-year-old study of U.S. Senate races Andrew Hacker concluded that

a divisive primary, in and of itself, bears little relation to a candidate's prospects at the general election. The sorts of candidates who win and lose are much the same in contests where one or neither or both of the contenders have first undergone a divisive primary.[5]

Twelve years later, using a slightly different operationalization of "divisiveness" and a larger slice of the historical record, Robert A. Bernstein found just the opposite. He concluded his study of U.S. Senate races by stating:

The data consistently support the thesis that divisive primaries reduce a candidate's prospects for winning the general election. Hacker contended that the apparent relationship between divisiveness and electoral success was spurious, that the real causes of success were incumbency and state party orientation. This analysis has shown that contention to be untrue. Even controlling for those variables, divisive primaries do hurt.[6]

The question, as it applies to presidential primaries, is whether divisiveness hurts either party's chances of winning those same states in the November general election. Table 29, which cross-tabulates the November results in presidential primary states by the presence or absence of divisiveness in one, both, or neither party's primaries, provides part of the answer.

Table 29 shows that for both parties, a divisive presidential primary in the spring increased the likelihood of the party losing that state in the fall. This relationship was particularly strong for the Democrats, who carried only four of the twenty-eight states in which they alone had had divisive primaries. Democratic prospects were also weakened, but not to the same degree, when both party primaries were hard-fought. When neither party's primaries were divisive, or when the Republicans alone had experienced divisiveness, the Democrats' success rate was highest.

Republicans were also weakened by divisive primaries, but not to the same degree. Over the five decades studied, the GOP's electoral prospects were weakest when it alone was exposed to divisive primaries, and weaker when neither party had a competitive contest in the spring. GOP prospects improved somewhat when both parties' primaries were contested, and the party enjoyed near invincibility when the Democrats alone fought it out in the preliminaries.

Up to this point, these findings mirror Hacker's and Bernstein's. Both found that candidates who face divisive primaries are more likely to

Table 29
Divisive Presidential Primaries and the Fate of the Party in Presidential Elections, 1932–1976

	DIVISIVE DEMOCRATIC ONLY	DIVISIVE BOTH PARTIES	DIVISIVE NEITHER PARTY	DIVISIVE REPUBLICAN ONLY
Democratic Victory	14% (4)	45% (5)	57% (76)	60% (15)
Republican Victory	86% (24)	55% (6)	43% (57)	40% (10)
	100%	100%	100%	100%
n =	(28)	(11)	(133)	(25)

SOURCE: *Presidential Elections Since 1789* 2d ed. (Washington, D.C.: Congressional Quarterly Inc., 1979), pp. 129–73.
NOTE: The 379 primaries in table 28 took place in the 197 states in table 29. From 1932 to 1976 there were 182 states which had primaries in both parties, and 15 states which had primaries in only one party for a total of 197 states and 379 primaries.

lose. Hacker, however, contends that losing is a function of incumbency and state party orientation. Bernstein, on the other hand, contends that the effect of divisive primaries still remains, even after controlling for both incumbency and state party orientation.

Incumbency

Intuitively, one might suspect that incumbency actually accounts for the relationship between divisiveness and electoral success or failure. The party out of office might be more likely to have divisive primaries since its nomination is open, and might also be more likely to lose general elections since it does not control the perquisites of the Oval Office. The party in office, on the other hand, because of the inherent powers of incumbents and incumbency, would have both fewer contested nominations and more general election success. The result over time would be the same: a large number of states would have experienced divisive primaries in one party (the out-party), and have voted for the other party (the in-party) in November. The explanation for a party's poor showing, however, would be incumbency, not divisiveness.

In order to test this possibility, Table 30 controls the general election behavior of divisive primary states by party incumbency.

As Table 30 shows, the effect of divisiveness remains even after con-

Table 30
**Divisive Presidential Primaries and the Fate of the Party in Presidential
Elections Controlled by Party Incumbency, 1932–1976**

DEMOCRATIC INCUMBENT

	Divisive Democratic Only	Divisive Both Parties	Divisive Neither Party	Divisive Republican Only
Democratic Victory	0% (0)	50% (1)	73% (54)	53% (10)
Republican Victory	100% (7)	50% (1)	27% (20)	47% (9)
	100%	100%	100%	100%
n =	(7)	(2)	(74)	(19)

REPUBLICAN INCUMBENT

	Divisive Democratic Only	Divisive Both Parties	Divisive Neither Party	Divisive Republican Only
Democratic Victory	19% (4)	44% (4)	37% (22)	83% (5)
Republican Victory	81% (17)	56% (5)	63% (37)	17% (1)
	100%	100%	100%	100%
n =	(21)	(9)	(59)	(6)

SOURCE: *Presidential Elections Since 1789* 2d ed. (Washington, D.C.: Congressional Quarterly Inc., 1979), pp. 129–73.

trolling for incumbency. Although it is true that divisive primaries are more prevalent in the out-party (76 percent of divisive Republican-only primaries occurred with a Democrat in office, and 75 percent of divisive Democratic-only primaries occurred with a Republican in office), the data still show that divisiveness exacts a toll on both incumbents and nonincumbents. When out of office, the Democrats lost 81 percent of the states which had experienced divisive Democratic-only primaries. As incumbents, they fared even worse. They lost 100 percent. When out of office, the Republicans lost 53 percent of those states which had experienced divisive Republican-only primaries. As incumbents, they lost 83 percent. In fact, both parties' prospects were bleakest when they were incumbents undergoing divisive nomination campaigns. Thus, for both parties, the power of incumbency reduces the likelihood of divisive contests, but it does not make either party immune to their effects.

State Party Orientation

Just as one could have suspected that incumbency created a spurious relationship between divisiveness and electoral success, one could also attribute the same effect to state party orientation. Since most delegate selection mechanisms in the past were tightly controlled by state and local party organizations, good party ties were usually a necessary precondition for a party nomination. If this was true, then presidential aspirants without strong organizational ties had only one strategy—to compete for delegates where their own party's organization was weakest. For Democratic aspirants, this meant competing in traditionally Republican states, and for Republican aspirants vice versa. The end result, of course, would be a large percentage of divisive Democratic presidential primaries in states which traditionally go Republican in the fall, and a large percentage of divisive Republican primaries in states which traditionally vote Democratic in the fall. This in turn would account for the apparent relationship between divisiveness and electoral failure.

Table 31 tests this possibility by controlling partisan choice of divisive primary states by the traditional party orientation of the state in presidential elections.[7] First, there is no indication from table 31 that divisive primaries were peculiar to opposition party strongholds. In direct contradiction to that argument, there were no divisive Republican primaries in traditionally Democratic states, and only 26 percent of all divisive Democratic primaries occurred in traditionally Republican states. Most divisive primaries, 54 percent of Democratic and 67 percent of Republican, occurred in states which were competitive at the presidential level.

Second, table 31 shows that in traditionally Democratic and competitive states, divisive primaries significantly weaken party prospects. The Democratic party is particularly hard-hit, winning only 38 percent of the traditionally Democratic states after a divisive Democratic-only primary, and winning none of the competitive states after a divisive primary in just the Democratic party. In competitive states the Republicans are also hurt significantly when a divisive primary is solely in their party, winning only 29 percent of the states under those conditions. In traditionally Republican states, divisive primaries weaken Democratic but not Republican prospects.

In general, then, divisive primaries do hurt. With the single exception

Table 31
Divisive Presidential Primaries and the Fate of the Party in Presidential Elections Controlled by State Party Orientation, 1932–1976

	TRADITIONALLY DEMOCRATIC			
	Divisive Demo Only	Divisive Both Parties	Divisive Neither Party	Divisive Rep Only
Democratic Victory	38% (3)	(0)	84% (26)	(0)
Republican Victory	63% (5)	(0)	16% (5)	(0)
	101%[a]		100%	
n =	(8)	(0)	(31)	(0)

	COMPETITIVE			
	Divisive Demo Only	Divisive Both Parties	Divisive Neither Party	Divisive Rep Only
Democratic Victory	0% (0)	43% (3)	50% (24)	71% (12)
Republican Victory	100% (14)	57% (4)	50% (24)	29% (5)
	100%	100%	100%	100%
n =	(14)	(7)	(48)	(17)

	TRADITIONALLY REPUBLICAN			
	Divisive Demo Only	Divisive Both Parties	Divisive Neither Party	Divisive Rep Only
Democratic Victory	17% (1)	50% (2)	48% (26)	37% (3)
Republican Victory	83% (5)	50% (2)	52% (28)	63% (5)
	100%	100%	100%	100%
n =	(6)	(4)	(54)	(8)

SOURCE: *Presidential Elections Since 1789* 2d ed. (Washington, D.C.: Congressional Quarterly Inc., 1979), pp. 129–73.

[a] Due to rounding.

of divisive Republican primaries in traditionally Republican states, divisive primaries significantly reduce the prospects of carrying the state in the presidential election regardless of incumbency or state party orientation.

DIVISIVE PRESIDENTIAL PRIMARIES AND DEFECTION IN GENERAL ELECTIONS

There are a number of ways divisiveness can hurt a party's chances in general elections. The losing contenders' supporters may not turn out in the general election, or they may vote for the other party's candidate. The losing contenders' workers may refuse to help or their contributors may refuse to donate to the eventual party nominee. Independents may be lured by the tranquility within the opposition party and repelled by the acrimony within the divided party. With the exception of the last factor, the common denominator of these explanations is the same: the development of candidate loyalties (from either ideological, issue, or stylistic affinities) which persist into the general election and override party loyalty as a determinant of electoral behavior. To date, only one of these potential explanations has been put to the empirical test. Donald Johnson and James Gibson found that divisiveness did produce a loss of campaign workers in November.[8] Using survey data collected in 1972 and 1976 a second explanation will be confirmed here: that supporters of losing contenders are more likely to defect in general elections.

In 1972 trial-heat questions were posed to each primary voter in the four states surveyed by the *New York Times*.[9] Richard Nixon (unopposed in his bid for renomination) was pitted against each of the Democratic contenders, and respondents were asked their presidential preference in each match-up. If candidate loyalties or antipathies which develop during divisive or competitive nomination campaigns are weaker than party identification, then Democratic primary voters should choose the Democratic nominee over Nixon in each pairing regardless of whether that Democratic contender was their personal choice in the primary. But, if candidate loyalties or antipathies are stronger, we should witness stronger support for Democratic nominees *from their own primary voters, and the backers of the losing contenders should be more inclined to defect.*

To illustrate, table 32 cross-tabulates the trial-heat presidential preference between Hubert Humphrey and Richard Nixon by Democrats who voted for Humphrey in the 1972 Florida primary and by Democrats whose loyalty rested with the six other Democratic presidential contenders. Table 32 shows that for this particular trial heat, candidate loyalty developed during the nomination stage would override party loyalty in the general election. Of Humphrey's voters in the Florida primary 85

Table 32
Trial-Heat Presidential Preference by Primary Vote of
Democrats in Florida, 1972

	HUMPHREY VOTERS IN PRIMARY	NON-HUMPHREY VOTERS IN PRIMARY[a]
Hubert Humphrey	85%	38%
Richard Nixon	14%	57%
	99%[b]	95%[b]
n =	(71)	(312)

SOURCE: Recomputed from 1972 *New York Times/Time/*Yankelovich, Skelly, and White, Inc. Primary Surveys

[a] Includes Wallace, Muskie, Chisholm, Lindsay, McGovern, and Jackson voters.

[b] Column totals do not add up to 100 percent because "not sure" category is omitted from the table. To compute the percentage of "not sures" subtract the column totals from 100 percent. In this case, one percent of the Humphrey voters and five percent of the non-Humphrey voters were unsure of their presidential preference given this particular pairing.

percent said they would vote for him in a Humphrey/Nixon contest in November, while only 14 percent said they would vote for Nixon. But among those Democrats who voted for the six other Democratic presidential contenders, the situation was far different. Only 38 percent claimed they would vote for the party's nominee, while 57 percent stated they would vote for Nixon.

Table 33 presents trial heats for each of the candidates in the four primaries surveyed. The "candidate loyalty" column for each state contains the presidential preference of Democratic voters whose primary choice is included in the pairing, that is, Humphrey voters in the Humphrey/Nixon pairing, McGovern voters in the McGovern/Nixon pairing. The "party loyalty" column contains the combined presidential vote intention of Democrats who voted for all other Democratic contenders in the primary (McGovern, Wallace, Muskie, Jackson, Lindsay, and Chisholm voters in the Humphrey/Nixon pairing in Florida; Humphrey, Wallace, Muskie, Jackson, Lindsay, and Chisholm voters in the McGovern/Nixon pairing, etc.).

The findings of every trial heat for all four states mirror the findings of the Humphrey/Nixon example. In every case party-loyalty scores were significantly lower than candidate-loyalty scores. In Florida, for instance, Nixon received more votes from the combined constituencies of the six hypothetical losers than did any hypothetical Democratic nominee. In the other three states Nixon also benefited, but not to the same degree. Depending on the nominee, the Republican incumbent picked up from 20 percent to 55 percent in Wisconsin, from 31 percent to 56 percent in Pennsylvania, and from 25 percent to 55 percent in Michigan. Since a losing constituency in these races comprises from 40 percent of a primary electorate in a two-candidate competitive primary to 80 percent in a multicandidate competitive primary, a defection rate even as low as 20 percent represents a substantial loss for the party.

In order to summarize the findings in table 33 and to facilitate interstate comparisons, statewide candidate-loyalty and party-loyalty scores were computed. This was done by weighting individual candidate- and party-loyalty scores by size of primary constituency, and then averaging the weighted scores of all candidates in a state.[10] Table 34 compares the statewide candidate- and party-loyalty scores in all four states.

As table 34 shows, candidate-loyalty scores exceeded party-loyalty scores by almost a two to one margin in three states and a three to one margin in one state. In all four states, primary voters showed staunch loyalty to the party if it nominated their first choice, and a strong propensity to defect if the party nod went to anyone else.

One problem with using trial heats during primaries is that attitudes, intentions, loyalties, and antipathies that developed then might be short-lived. The presidential election takes place three to six months later and this allows sufficient time for loyalties and antipathies to die and for party loyalty to reemerge. The question of course is whether they do. Returning to the 1972 California Poll and introducing the 1976 American National Election Study will help shed some light on this question.[11]

In 1972 the Field Corporation conducted a post-election survey of the California presidential electorate,[12] and in 1976 the Center for Political Studies conducted a post-election survey of the national presidential electorate.[13] Since the California primary was hotly contested in 1972 (the Humphrey/McGovern showdown), since both parties had competitive campaigns for nomination in 1976, and since both sets of post-election respondents were asked about their primary vote, both surveys can be used to determine whether defection in general elections was actually related to candidate loyalty in primaries. Table 35, which cross-tabulates presidential vote by primary vote for California in 1972 and for the nation in 1976, provides the answer.

Table 35 shows that in 1972 and 1976 disaffection over the party's presidential nominee persisted into the general election, and the result

Table 33

Candidate-Loyalty and Party-Loyalty Scores of Four 1972 Democratic Presidential Primary Electorates

	FLORIDA N = (383)		WISCONSIN N = (187)[a]		PENNSYLVANIA N = (414)		MICHIGAN N = (221)[a]	
	Candidate Loyalty	*Party Loyalty*	*Candidate Loyalty*	*Party Loyalty*	*Candidate Loyalty*	*Party Loyalty*	*Candidate Loyalty*	*Party Loyalty*
Humphrey	85%	38%	100%	72%	90%	61%	94%	58%
Nixon	14%	57%	0%	20%	10%	31%	6%	28%
	99%	95%	100%	92%	100%	92%	100%	86%
McGovern	92%	34%	99%	69%	97%	56%	90%	67%
Nixon	8%	52%	2%	22%	2%	31%	4%	25%
	100%	86%	101%	91%	99%	87%	94%	92%
Wallace	87%	13%	82%	21%	89%	22%	94%	23%
Nixon	12%	75%	9%	55%	12%	56%	4%	55%
	99%	88%	91%	76%	101%	78%	98%	78%

Muskie	92%	43%	[b]100%	71%	90%	56%
Nixon	6%	50%	0%	21%	6%	34%
	98%	93%	100%	92%	96%	90%
Jackson	71%	35%	[c]100%	57%		
Nixon	23%	47%	0%	30%		
	94%	82%	100%	87%		
Lindsay	88%	32%				
Nixon	12%	61%				
	100%	93%				
Chisholm	94%	16%				
Nixon	6%	75%				
	100%	91%				

SOURCE: Recomputed from 1972 *New York Times*/*Time*/Yankelovich, Skelly, and White, Inc. Primary Surveys

[a] Since Wisconsin and Michigan were open primary states in 1972, I computed party-loyalty and candidate-loyalty scores for *Democrats* only. This explains the smaller N's and eliminates any artificial inflation of scores due to Republicans voting in Democratic primaries.

[b] p = < .01

[c] p = < .05

For all other trial heats, p = < .001

Table 34
Weighted Candidate- and Party-Loyalty
Scores of Four Democratic Presidential
Primary Electorates

	CANDIDATE-LOYALTY SCORE	PARTY-LOYALTY SCORE
Florida	84%	26%
Wisconsin	96%	58%
Pennsylvania	92%	50%
Michigan	93%	42%

SOURCE: Recomputed from 1972 *New York Times/Time*/Yankelovich, Skelly, and White, Inc. Primary Surveys

was as predicted—widespread defection. In California in 1972, 87 percent of McGovern's primary voters preferred him over Richard Nixon in the presidential election, while only 14 percent defected. The Democrats who supported the other Democratic contenders in the primary, however, were never recaptured: 50 percent voted for Nixon, while only 45 percent remained loyal to their party. Also, note the close similarity between the actual candidate- (87) and party-loyalty (45) scores in California and the projected scores in Florida, Wisconsin, Pennsylvania, and Michigan (table 34).

In 1976, as in 1972, primary supporters of the eventual nominee displayed strong loyalty toward their candidate in the presidential election. Jimmy Carter received 85 percent of the vote of his primary voters, while losing only 16 percent. The supporters of the losing contenders were almost three times more disloyal: 55 percent voted for Carter, while the remaining 46 percent voted for the three other candidates in the race.

The extent to which candidate loyalties weaken the Democratic party's electoral prospects will vary from year to year. Candidate loyalties should be strongest, party loyalties should be weakest, and party prospects should be slimmest in an election year like 1972, when the Democratic nomination was open and competitive and when a Republican breezed through the preliminaries unscathed.

In a year like 1976, when both parties had competitive or divisive nominating campaigns, Democratic prospects increased somewhat since Democratic defections were, to some extent, offset by Republican defections. Table 35 shows that Republican defection in the 1976 presidential election was also related to candidate choice in primaries: 86 percent of

Table 35

Actual Candidate- and Party-Loyalty Scores in California in 1972 and Nationwide in 1976

	DEMOCRATIC CALIFORNIA 1972			DEMOCRATIC NATIONWIDE 1976			REPUBLICAN NATIONWIDE 1976	
	Candidate Loyalty	*Party Loyalty[a]*		*Candidate Loyalty*	*Party Loyalty[b]*		*Candidate Loyalty*	*Party Loyalty[c]*
McGovern	87%	45%	Carter	85%	55%	Carter	86%	73%
Nixon	13%	50%	Ford	13%	39%	Ford	9%	24%
Other	1%	4%	Others[d]	3%	7%	Others[d]	5%	4%
	101%[e]	99%[e]		101%[e]	101%[e]		100%	101%[e]
n =	(157)	(141)		(155)	(82)		(123)	(67)

SOURCE: California Poll 7207, Field Research Corporation, San Francisco, Ca. and CPS 1976 American National Election Study (ICPSR Study 7381), Inter-University Consortium for Political and Social Research, University of Michigan, Ann Arbor, Michigan.

[a] Humphrey, Wallace, Chisholm, Muskie, Yorty, and McCarthy primary voters

[b] Bayh, Brown, Harris, Humphrey, Jackson, McCormack, Shapp, Udall, Wallace, and Church primary voters. (Democrats only)

[c] Reagan primary voters. (Republicans only)

[d] McCarthy, Maddox

[e] Due to rounding

Ford's Republican primary voters stuck by him in the general election while only 14 percent defected. Reagan Republicans, on the other hand, were twice as disloyal: 73 percent supported Ford, while 28 percent defected to the three other candidates in the race. On balance, however, the Democratic party still suffered a net loss when both parties subjected their followers to competitive campaigns. Because of the more diverse ideological base of the Democratic party, the percentage of disgruntled Democrats should always exceed the percentage of disgruntled Republicans. In addition, since Democrats outnumber Republicans two to one, the absolute number of dissatisfied Democrats should always exceed the absolute number of dissatisfied Republicans, even given equal party loyalty scores for both parties. Democratic party prospects should be strongest when little or no competition exists for the party nomination.

It is also interesting to note that the generalizations about Democratic and Republican electoral prospects drawn from survey data neatly match the historical state level data presented in table 29 (p. 87). Democratic losses and Republican gains at the state level are greatest, just as Democratic losses and Republican gains on the individual level are greatest, when only the Democratic party experiences competitive nomination campaigns. Democratic losses and Republican gains at the state level decrease, just as individual net losses and gains decrease, when both parties' nominations are hard-fought. Democratic party prospects are brightest and Republican party prospects are bleakest when either competition is removed from both parties' nomination stage or the Republican party alone is plagued by divisiveness.

In addition, these findings reveal something about presidential primaries often missed by students of American government. In most studies of presidential elections, primaries are treated as part of the environment with which only presidential contenders must deal. But primaries are also an important part of the environment for voters. Primaries shape and mold voters' attitudes and opinions toward candidates and issues, and these images do not necessarily disappear after the primary. They remain with the voters and form part of the mind-set that influences general election behavior. To ignore primaries when studying general elections is to ignore a dynamic relationship that increases our understanding of both.

OPEN VERSUS CLOSED PRESIDENTIAL PRIMARIES

The question of who should be allowed to vote in presidential primaries has divided Democratic party leaders since the advent of primaries over seventy years ago. Some party leaders advocate open primaries, or primaries in which Republicans and Independents as well as Democrats can vote. Others, whose views probably represent majority opinion within the party, argue for closed primaries or for restricting the vote to Democrats only.

One reason why party leaders have failed either to abolish or endorse open primaries is because informed judgments are difficult to make when very little empirical information exists about them. Claims of "raiding" are often made by opponents of open primaries, but such claims are usually conjectures. The real effects of opening one's nomination process to the followers of the opposition party still remain somewhat of a mystery.

Some degree of insight into open primaries may result from an examination of the partisan composition of the 1972 Wisconsin and Michigan Democratic primaries and of the candidate choice of those partisans. Table 36 shows that the partisan composition of the Wisconsin and Michigan primary electorates were very similar.

In both states, Democrats composed the largest single contingent of primary voters; Independents, the second largest, and Republicans, the smallest. The more significant and alarming finding, though, is the presence of a large number of non-Democrats. In Wisconsin, Independents and Republicans actually formed a majority of voters in the Democratic primary. In Michigan, nearly one out of every two primary voters did not consider himself to be a Democrat.

It should be noted that although both parties held presidential primaries in Wisconsin and Michigan in 1972 only the Democratic primary was competitive. Thus, the large number of Republicans and Independents in the Democratic primary could be explained by the ab-

Table 36
Partisan Composition of Open Democratic
Presidential Primaries in Wisconsin and
Michigan—1972

	WISCONSIN	MICHIGAN
Democratic	49%	54%
Independent	42%	40%
Republican	9%	6%
	100%	100%
n =	382	410

SOURCE: Recomputed from 1972 *New York Times/ Time*/Yankelovich, Skelly, and White, Inc. Primary Surveys

sence of a meaningful Republican contest. In open primaries where both parties have important contests the number of intruders should be smaller.

By itself, the presence of large numbers of outsiders in Democratic primaries does not create any problems. Problems emerge only if the candidate preferences of non-Democrats differ from the candidate preferences of Democrats, because only then do Republicans and Independents influence the outcomes of primary elections, and thus the political fate of Democratic contenders and the constituents and the policies with which they are associated.

Partisan-related candidate preferences can result by design or by accident. In the former case, Republicans might deliberately cast ballots for the Democrat whom they perceive to be the weakest opponent in November. In the latter case, Democrats, Independents, and Republicans might be personally attracted by the different styles or policy promises of different Democratic contenders. Regardless of explanation, the effect of partisan-related candidate preferences is to distort both the voice of party members and the strength of the party's presidential contenders.

The 1972 Wisconsin Democratic primary was a major turning point in the 1972 campaign. Senator George McGovern won with 31 percent of the vote and the victory reinvigorated his slumping campaign. Senator Hubert Humphrey finished second with 22 percent of the vote. Governor George Wallace finished a close third with 21 percent of the vote. In order to determine whether opening the Wisconsin primary to Republicans and Independents had any effect on the outcome, table 37 cross-tabulates candidate choice by party identification.

As table 37 shows, whether the reason was style, issues, or partisan plot, support for the three major candidates varied by party, with each group of partisans preferring a different Democratic contender. Wisconsin Democrats preferred Hubert Humphrey. They gave him 32 percent of their vote compared to 29 percent for McGovern and only 15 percent for Wallace. Unfortunately for Humphrey, the primary was open and Democrats composed only 49 percent of the electorate. Had the primary been closed to Independents and Republicans, Humphrey undoubtedly would have won.[14] George McGovern, on the other hand, the winner in Wisconsin, was the first choice of Wisconsin Independents. He received 34 percent of their vote, compared to Wallace's 22 percent, and Humphrey's 14 percent. George Wallace was the overwhelming choice of Wisconsin Republicans. In their voting, Republicans favored Wallace over McGovern by almost two to one, and Wallace over Humphrey by eleven to one.

An open Democratic presidential primary was also held in the state of

Table 37
Candidate Choice by Party Identification in the 1972 Wisconsin
Democratic Presidential Primary

	DEMOCRATS	INDEPENDENTS	REPUBLICANS
Humphrey	32%	14%	4%
McGovern	29%	34%	23%
Wallace	15%	22%	44%
Others[a]	24%	29%	30%
	100%	99%[b]	101%[b]

SOURCE: Recomputed from 1972 *New York Times/Time/*Yankelovich, Skelly, and
White, Inc. Primary Surveys
[a] Chisholm, Jackson, Lindsay, Muskie, others
[b] Due to rounding

Michigan. George Wallace won the Michigan primary with 51 percent of
the vote. George McGovern finished second with 27 percent of the vote.
Hubert Humphrey finished third with 16 percent. Table 38 cross-
tabulates candidate choice by party in that state's open primary.

The findings in Michigan were similar. Humphrey's major source of
support was derived from Democrats, McGovern's was derived from
Independents leaning Democratic, and Wallace's was derived from Independents, Independents leaning Republican, and Republicans. Although a closed primary would not have reversed or even changed the
order of finish, it would have narrowed the gap considerably. Just as in

Table 38
Candidate Choice by Party Identification in the 1972 Michigan
Democratic Presidential Primary

	DEMO	IND. DEMO	IND	IND. REP	REP
Humphrey	26%	4%	4%	0%	9%
McGovern	29%	46%	17%	9%	7%
Wallace	39%	41%	76%	87%	79%
Others[a]	6%	9%	4%	4%	5%
	100%	100%	101%[b]	100%	100%

SOURCE: Recomputed from 1972 *New York Times/Time/*Yankelovich, Skelly, and
White, Inc. Primary Surveys
[a] Muskie, others
[b] Due to rounding

Wisconsin, Hubert Humphrey would have benefited most from a primary restricted to Democrats. His percentage of the vote would have jumped from 16 percent to 26 percent. George McGovern would also have benefited, but only slightly. His 27 percent of the vote would have increased to 29 percent. George Wallace, on the other hand, because of his strong Republican and Independent support would have lost considerable ground. His 24 percentage point lead over McGovern (51%–27%) would have dropped to 10 percentage points (39%–29%), and his 35 percentage point bulge over Humphrey (51%–16%) would have shrunk to only 13 percentage points (39%–26%). Of course, a closed primary would have also changed each candidate's share of the state delegation accordingly, with Humphrey's share increasing, Wallace's decreasing, and McGovern's remaining about the same.

The presence of Independents and Republicans in these two Democratic presidential primaries distorted in a major way the appeal of all three Democratic contenders. In both states, the strongest Democratic contender was weakened and the weakest contender was strengthened. Such a distortion is acceptable if there is reason for testing each contender's appeal among Republicans and Independents. In other words, if the Democratic party was the minority party, strong *interparty* appeal might be important, since victory in the general election could be had only with large Republican defections. The Democratic party, however, is the majority party, and it does not need Republican defections. Victory is assured by the nomination of someone with strong *intraparty* appeal. Moreover, Republican support in primaries is no guarantee of Republican support in presidential elections. By the time the nominees square off in November, Republicans may well be back in their own party's camp.

The explanation for the partisan-related candidate preferences in Wisconsin and Michigan was probably style or issues rather than an organized Republican raid. First, in both primaries, the number of Republican voters was small. An organized Republican attempt to influence the outcome of the election would have produced a larger Republican turnout, especially given the absence of a contest in their own primary. In addition, the massive mobilization required to carry out such a raid would have attracted publicity, but none was in evidence at the time. Second, the candidate preference of each partisan group was consistent with the ideological position of that group. Traditional party identifiers would have found the New Deal philosophy of Hubert Humphrey to their liking. Issue liberals, who have come more and more to identify themselves as Independents in recent years, would have preferred George McGovern. Republicans would have surely shared many of George Wallace's conservative views. All of this, of course, assumes some degree of ideological voting in primaries, which is one aspect of the following, broader consideration.

CANDIDATE CHOICE IN PRESIDENTIAL PRIMARIES

Over the years a great deal of research has been devoted to the question of what influences voters' candidate choices.[15] From these studies, three variables have been discovered. By far, the most important determinant of the vote is party identification. It explains about 70 percent of all candidate preferences in the seven presidential elections through 1976, and no other variable comes close to matching its predictive power. The other two variables, candidate image and issues, are much less powerful, although studies have discovered an increase in the level of issue voting over the past decade.[16]

Unfortunately, party identification is irrelevant to the study of candidate choice in closed primaries since voters and candidates are members of the same party. In fact, the limited utility of party identification becomes evident when thinking in terms of primaries. Assuming two primary elections for every general election, party identification is inconsequential to the vote decision in two-thirds of all U.S. elections. Yet in every one of those primaries, Democrats are faced with the task of choosing among contenders, a task made more difficult by the presence of large numbers of presidential aspirants. How do they decide? In 1972, ideology played a significant role in their decision-making process. Table 39 cross-tabulates candidate choice by the ideological self-identification of Democratic voters in Florida's 1972 presidential primary.

Table 39 shows that as early as the second primary, and even within an extremely large field, candidate choice was linked to ideological self-identification.[17] McGovern's, Lindsay's, Muskie's, and Chisholm's support rested almost exclusively with liberal Florida Democrats. McGovern received 15 percent of the liberal vote, but only 5 percent of the moderate vote and 2 percent of the conservative vote. Lindsay received 19 percent of the liberal vote, but only 6 percent of the moderate vote and 3 percent of the conservative vote. Muskie received 18 percent of the liberal vote, but only 8 percent of the moderate vote and 6 percent of the conservative vote. Interestingly enough, by any objective standards one could devise, all four of these candidates were indeed the most liberal contenders in the Florida primary.

George Wallace, on the other hand, was correctly perceived by conservative self-identifiers as being their type of candidate. The Alabama governor received 55 percent of the conservative vote and only 14 percent of the liberal vote.

The votes for Hubert Humphrey and Henry Jackson reflect the typical

Table 39
Candidate Preferences by Ideological Self-Identification of Democrats in Florida—1972

	LIBERAL	MODERATE	CONSERVATIVE
McGovern	15%	5%	2%
Lindsay	19%	6%	3%
Muskie	18%	8%	6%
Chisholm	5%	4%	1%
Jackson	14%	15%	13%
Humphrey	16%	19%	20%
Wallace	14%	41%	55%
Others[a]	0%	2%	0%
	101%[b]	100%	100%

SOURCE: Recomputed from 1972 *New York Times/Time/*Yankelovich, Skelly, and White, Inc. Primary Surveys

[a] Muskie, others
[b] Due to rounding

problem of centrist candidates in multicandidate fields. They managed to be either second or third choices of all three ideological blocs, but favorites of none. Their strength, which emerges only in individual match-ups with candidates of the right or left, dissipates quickly in multicandidate contests.

As table 40 shows, the relationship between candidate choice and ideological self-identification in Wisconsin, Pennsylvania, and Michigan was similar to that in Florida. In all three states, George McGovern, the liberal in the race, was the favorite of liberal Democrats. He captured nearly one out of every two liberal votes in Wisconsin and Michigan, and one out of every three liberal votes in Pennsylvania. His percentage of the liberal vote in Wisconsin, Pennsylvania, and Michigan exceeded his percentage of the conservative vote by increasing margins of two to one, three to one, and four to one, respectively. George Wallace's support, on the other hand, centered among conservative Democrats. In all three states, his percentage of the conservative vote more than doubled his percentage of the liberal vote. Hubert Humphrey again had the broadest ideological following. He was the second choice of both liberals and conservatives in all three states, and the first choice of moderates in two of the three states.

In California, Mervin Field also used an ideological self-identification scale.[18] The findings in California, as shown in table 41, also attest to the role of ideology, in some fashion, as an integral part of primary election decision making.

Table 40
Candidate Preferences by Ideological Self-Identification of Democrats in Wisconsin, Pennsylvania, Michigan—1972

	WISCONSIN			PENNSYLVANIA			MICHIGAN		
	Lib	Mod	Con	Lib	Mod	Con	Lib	Mod	Con
McGovern	43%	23%	21%	33%	17%	11%	51%	25%	11%
Humphrey	30%	30%	37%	30%	33%	35%	17%	31%	27%
Wallace	8%	17%	20%	14%	23%	30%	25%	39%	55%
Others[a]	19%	29%	21%	23%	27%	24%	7%	5%	7%
	100%	99%[b]	99%[b]	100%	100%	100%	100%	100%	100%

SOURCE: Recomputed from 1972 *New York Times/Time*/Yankelovich, Skelly, and White, Inc. Primary Surveys

[a] Muskie, Lindsay, Jackson, Chisholm, others

[b] Due to rounding

Table 41

Candidate Preferences by Ideological Self-Identification of Democrats in California—1972

	STRONG LIBERAL	MILD LIBERAL	MIDDLE OF THE ROAD	MILD CONSERV	STRONG CONSERV
McGovern	81%	60%	54%	40%	29%
Humphrey	8%	23%	32%	38%	29%
Wallace	0%	6%	7%	11%	43%
Others[a]	12%	11%	7%	11%	0%
	101%[b]	100%	100%	100%	101%[b]

SOURCE: California Poll 7204, Field Research Corporation, San Francisco, Calif.
[a] Chisholm, Jackson, McCarthy, Muskie, others
[b] Due to rounding

George McGovern's support in California was strongly related to the ideological self-identification of Democrats. From strong liberals and mild liberals he received 81 percent and 60 percent of the vote, respectively. From mild conservatives and strong conservatives he received only 40 percent and 29 percent of the vote. George Wallace was again the favorite of strongly conservative Democrats, capturing two out of their every five votes as a write-in candidate. Hubert Humphrey's support in California, as it was in the four preceding primaries, was concentrated among moderate Democrats.

That a relationship between candidate choice and ideological self-identification exists in presidential primaries is probably a function of four factors. First, as noted in chapter 2, primary electorates tend to be skewed toward the upper end of the SES scale, and upper-SES individuals tend to be more issue-conscious and ideologically aware. Hence, primary electorates tend to exhibit more ideological sophistication than either the general election electorate or the party membership as a whole. Second, some primary voters might rely on simple ideological labels in much the same way they rely on simple party labels. During the course of the campaign, the press is quick to point out ideological differences between the candidates in rather simple, straightforward, and nonissue terms, such as, "Udall, the liberal in the race..." Unable to differentiate between the issue positions and policy promises of a large number of contenders all of whom are Democrats and all of whom sound alike except to the well-trained political ear, voters might simply adopt ideological labels themselves in response to the campaign and then choose the candidate whose label corresponds to their own. Third, primary voters might adopt the ideological label of a candidate whom they have chosen on some other grounds, for example, style or charisma. And fourth, the press may have succeeded in giving these labels real meaning for the mass public, especially in years like 1968 and 1972 when major ideological differences did appear during the nomination stage. Regardless of reason, the relationship between ideological self-identification and candidate choice confirms the earlier findings: presidential primaries bestow benefits upon certain candidates, interests, and factions within the Democratic party, and in addition, provides a foundation upon which to build an explanation of candidate choice in presidential primaries.

NOTES

1. To be considered a presidential contender, a candidate must have received over 1 percent of the vote in at least two presidential primaries during the year in which he sought the nomination. The 1 percent/two primary criterion established a minimum level of competitiveness and prevented "crank" candidates (e.g., Edward Coll in 1968, Arthur O'Blessit in 1972) from making the list. Yet this minimum was still low enough so that it did not exclude legitimate long-shot possibilities who saw the post-Reform changes as their personal ticket to the White House. It is also interesting to note that the absence of "crank" candidates in earlier years and their presence in more recent years also attested to the permeability of the new system.

While it is true that in the past there were serious candidates who did not go the primary route (now all do), it is also true that most serious candidates since 1932 satisfied this minimum threshold.

The main sources for the primary returns are Louise Overacker, *Presidential Elections* (New York: Macmillan, 1926); James Davis, *Presidential Primaries: Road to the White House* (New York: Thomas Y. Crowell Co., 1967); Walter Kravits, *Presidential Preference Primaries, 1928–1956* (Washington, D.C.: Library of Congress, 1960) and *Presidential Elections Since 1789* (Washington, D.C.: Congressional Quarterly, 1979).

2. As shown below, the same trends were obtained by using a 5 percent/two primary criterion:

	TOTAL NUMBER OF CONTENDERS	AVERAGE NUMBER PER ELECTION YEAR
Roosevelt era (1932–1948)	10	2.0
Pre-Reform era (1952–1968)	17	3.4
Post-Reform era (1972–1976)	18	9.0

Source: *Presidential Elections Since 1789* 2d ed. (Washington, D.C.: Congressional Quarterly Inc., 1979), pp. 129–73.

3. The 20 percent margin of victory is identical to Robert Bernstein's measure of divisiveness in "Divisive Primaries Do Hurt: U.S. Senate Races, 1956–1972," *American Political Science Review* 71 (June 1977): 540.

A 50,000 vote cutoff was used since it was high enough to prevent all but the most competitive write-in primaries from being included, and since it was low enough so that all presidential primaries which were held in less-populated states (e.g., New Hampshire), and which met the 20 percent margin, would be included.

Where data were unavailable, or where candidates' names did not appear on the ballot, competitiveness could not be determined, and the states were not included in the analysis. In 1972 data were unavailable for Alabama and Arkansas, and contenders' names did not appear on the ballot in New York. In 1976 data were unavailable for Texas and Alabama, and the names of the contenders did not appear on the ballot in New York. The District of Columbia and all U.S. territories are excluded from the analysis.

4. Andrew Hacker, "Does a 'Divisive' Primary Harm a Candidate's Election Chances," *American Political Science Review* 59 (March 1965): 105–10; Robert A. Bernstein, "Divisive Primaries Do Hurt: U.S. Senate Races, 1956–1972," *American Political Science Review* 71 (June 1977): 540–45; and Donald Johnson and James Gibson, "The Divisive Primary Revisited: Party Activists in Iowa," *American Political Science Review* 68 (March 1974): 67–77.

5. Hacker, "Does a 'Divisive' Primary Harm a Candidate's Election Chances," p. 110.

6. Bernstein, 'Divisive Primaries Do Hurt," p. 544.

7. States whose Democratic percentage in each of three presidential elections immediately prior to the year of the primary exceeded the national Democratic average were categorized "traditionally Democratic." States whose Republican percentage in those three elections exceeded the national Republican average were categorized "traditionally Republican." States which split their partisan loyalties were categorized "competitive."

This measure is an attempt to capture a state's orientation or leaning at the presidential level and not its orientation as a whole (local, state, and national). Since our principal concern is presidential elections, and since many states have one orientation at the state and local level and another at the presidential level (e.g., southern states) it would make very little sense to incorporate state and local voting habits in the measure. Also, since "tradition" does not preclude the possibility of change, and since state presidential traditions have changed over time (the south), the number of presidential elections was limited to three. Admittedly, three elections is an arbitrary choice, but so would be two or four. The advantage to using three is that it is more likely to capture change across time without stacking the deck (more than three elections would make many southern states, which are now Republican, either Democratic or competitive).

8. Johnson and Gibson, "Divisive Primaries Revisited," pp. 67–77.

9. 1972 *New York Times/Time*/Yankelovich, Skelly, and White, Inc. primary surveys.

10. A simple statewide average was not used since minor candidates with high candidate-loyalty scores and low party-loyalty scores (e.g., Chisholm in

Florida) would unfairly inflate the defection and support scores. Weighting by size of constituency gives a more accurate estimation of probable statewide support and defection rates since it sensitizes the scores to each candidate's actual strength within the primary electorate.

11. The national data utilized in this section were made available by the Inter-University Consortium for Political and Social Research (ICPSR Study 7381), P.O. Box 1248, Ann Arbor, Michigan, 48104. The data for the CPS 1976 American National Election Study were originally collected by the Center for Political Studies (CPS) of the Institute for Social Research, the University of Michigan under a grant from the National Science Foundation. Neither the original collectors of the data nor the Consortium bear any responsibility for the analyses or interpretations presented here.

12. California Poll 7207, Field Research Corporation, San Francisco, Ca.

13. ICPSR Study 7381, Inter-University Consortium for Political and Social Research, P.O. Box 1248, Ann Arbor, Michigan, 48104.

14. This assumes no changes in party identification or turnout given a closed primary.

15. Angus Campbell et al. *The American Voter* (New York: John Wiley and Sons, 1960); Donald E. Stokes, "Some Dynamic Elements of Contests for the Presidency," *American Political Science Review* 60 (March 1966): 12–28; V. O. Key, *The Responsible Electorate* (Cambridge, Mass.: Harvard University Press, 1966); David RePass, "Issue Salience and Party Choice," *American Political Science Review* 65 (June 1971): 389–400; Gerald M. Pomper, "From Confusion to Clarity: Issues and American Voters, 1956–1968," *American Political Science Review* 66 (June 1972): 415–28; Norman H. Nie, Sidney Verba, and John Petrocik, *The Changing American Voter* (Cambridge, Mass.: Harvard University Press, 1976).

16. RePass, "Issue Salience and Party Choice"; Pomper, "From Confusion to Clarity"; Nie, *Changing American Voter*.

For an excellent summary of past and present controversies in voting behavior, *see* Richard G. Niemi and Herbert Weisberg, *Controversies in American Voting Behavior* (San Francisco: W. H. Freeman, 1976).

17. In Florida, a fourth category called "radical" was included in the ideological self-identification question. Since radical denotes both right- and left-wing ideology, it was eliminated from table 39. An indication that it was interpreted that way in Florida is evidenced by the candidate choices of radicals. Wallace received 35 percent of the radical vote and Chisholm received 38 percent.

18. California Poll 7204, Field Research Corporation, San Francisco, Ca.

7

THE DEMOCRATIC PARTY IN THE POST-REFORM ERA

A NOMINATION system based heavily or exclusively on presidential primaries creates a unique problem for a low-SES, majority party like the Democratic party. Membership of the Democratic party tends to be predominantly lower-SES. However, the composition of Democratic primary electorates tends to be predominantly upper-SES since turnout in presidential primaries is strongly related to socioeconomic status. That a minority of rich and better-educated Democrats exercises disproportionate influence over candidate decisions, and consequently over public policy, would prove to be of little political significance if all Democrats, regardless of socioeconomic standing, tended to think or behave alike or if all Democrats acted out of party interest (instead of ideological interest) when casting their primary ballots. Unfortunately, neither was the case in California in 1968 and 1972. Issue concerns, ideological perspectives, and candidate preferences varied by socioeconomic status within the party, and presidential contenders were differentiated within primary electorates to a large degree by their ideology or ideological labels, not by their ability to win elections. The result was primary electorates with political orientations far different from the party membership as a whole, and primary voters who, unlike the decision makers of the past (professional politicians in old-fashioned party caucuses), placed ideological interests above party interests when choosing their presidential nominee.

The immediate and long-term implications for the Democratic party are serious, depending on the extent to which these patterns are repeated every four years. In the short run, and depending on election-year issues and the degree to which they polarize the party along class lines similar to those found in 1968 and 1972, unrepresentative primary electorates could lead to minority-based nominees (i.e., New Politics or Southern) or to nominees who must keep their policy preference vague in order to appeal both to New Politics and Southern constituencies. In either case, the short-term result is the same, either Republican presidents (when the Democratic nominee comes from the New Politics faction) or Democratic presidents who are indistinguishable from their Republican counterparts—presidents who might as well be Republican (when the nominee comes from the Southern faction).

In the medium run, party policy and party candidates could come more and more to reflect the political, social, and economic interests of those Democrats who participate in the nomination process, interests which are, for the most part, noticeably different from those of traditional party supporters and general election participants. The latter, locked out of their party's most important decision-making process, and disturbed by the gradual but noticeable shift in party policy, will begin to look elsewhere. Faced with a choice between a moderate Republican and either a New Politics nominee or a vague and ambiguous nominee, these traditional party supporters may well opt for the Republican, only to return to their traditional party allegiance once the election is over. When faced with similar choices over a series of elections, they will begin to find it more and more difficult to return. While such voters get to stave off whatever they regard as the greater of two evils, they do not receive much hope of obtaining the kind of governmental policies which they would prefer.

Over the long run, this pattern could have even more destabilizing, and pernicious, consequences. As such a statistically large group is forced to waver, election-in and election-out, between choices which it cannot view as attractive, the ability of the entire political system to deliver policy outcomes that are in line with public wishes might decline precipitously. More frequent Republican or "do-nothing Democratic" presidents will still face traditional Democratic Congresses, and stalemate is the most likely result. Over time, the situation could presumably grow worse, rather than better, because the groups which are most unhappy at the presidential election level will have less incentive to participate at all, and their declining participation will only exacerbate the trend at that level. On the other hand, a successful Republican party effort to moderate its economic and social welfare position might be sufficient to turn these series of one-night stands into a more permanent arrangement, and to convert the Republican party into the de facto majority party, first at the national level, then locally as well—in the process resolving the prior instability and creating a new partisan alignment in American politics.

If recent changes in the nomination process are gradually shifting control within the Democratic party from one set of constituents to another, and from one set of party leaders to another; if they are also shifting party concern from one set of issues to another; and if, in the process, this transformation is lowering rather than raising the party's electoral prospects, what can be done?

Since changes in the delegate selection process seem to be partly responsible for this trend, perhaps they can also afford a cure. Over the years, delegates to the national convention have been chosen by three different methods—old-fashioned party caucuses, participatory conventions, and presidential primaries. Since participation under all three plans falls short of 100 percent, and is uniformly related to socioeconomic status, all three methods produce bodies of decision makers which are demographically unrepresentative of the party membership. But since the number of participants varies by delegate selection method, the amount of demographic unrepresentativeness should also vary.

Despite their inherent unrepresentativeness, primary election voters are probably more demographically representative of the party membership than either activists in participatory conventions or party professionals in old-fashioned party caucuses. Primary turnout is higher than either convention or caucus turnout, and higher turnouts normally produce greater degrees of demographic representation. Thus, if more demographic representation were all one sought in a delegate-selection system, presidential primaries would still have to be considered the lesser of three evils.

Contrary to common belief, however, marginal increases in demographic representativeness do not necessarily guarantee marginal increases in party responsiveness, that is, in nominees and policies more in accord with rank-and-file views and preferences. Decisions made in primaries (and for that matter, decisions made in participatory conventions) only reflect the interests of those who turn out. Primaries cannot, because of their simple referendum nature, take into account the views of those who fail to get to the polls. But when primary no-shows are in fact the heart of the party membership and the bulk of its presidential electorate, failure to consider or respond to their needs and interests becomes both a structural problem and, more importantly, a central concern of democratic politics.

On the other hand, old-fashioned party caucuses, where participation is limited to, and decisions are made by, party leaders are probably less demographically representative of the party membership than primary electorates. However, these caucuses may well be capable of much greater responsiveness. Since the nomination is viewed by party leaders as a means to an end—with the end being victory in the general election—party leaders are forced to push the types of programs and to choose the types of candidates that appeal, not to themselves (as activists in participatory conventions and voters in presidential primaries are encouraged to do), but to the party membership and to the presidential electorate. In many cases, the desire on the part of party leadership to attain this end (electoral victory) is reinforced by a desire to retain the perquisites of office, or the policy controls which go with it. In other cases, it is reinforced by the desire to get along with the predominant social interests in the leader's home area, or by the fact that the leader himself comes out of, and implicitly represents, those interests. But in almost all cases, the party leadership is likely to have had the types of experiences which make it fully sensitive to what will and will not prove attractive to their constituents. In short, party responsiveness and rank-and-file control is furthered in old-fashioned party caucuses by the social pressures on party leadership, and, behind them, by partisan competition.[1] Neither of these mechanisms is as direct as participatory conventions or presidential primaries, for example, but both are nevertheless very powerful. In contrast, only the illusion of control and responsiveness is present in presidential primaries and participatory conventions, an illusion perpetuated by the beneficiaries of those systems.

Unfortunately, even those who judge the party caucus to be the method most responsive to party followers and best able to produce a winner must doubt whether it remains a viable option. Old-fashioned party caucuses assume old-fashioned political parties, and the latter have been in decline for forty years even if they cannot be totally counted out in many areas. Beyond that, the history of party reform is not encouraging to those who might want to return to earlier structural devices; old methods are rarely recycled. Finally, and most importantly, those who benefit from the growth of primaries are also less likely to be willing to endorse "non-Reform" procedures.

If the problems associated with the unrepresentativeness of primary electorates cannot be eliminated by a full-scale restructuring of the delegate-selection process, they can, at least potentially, be minimized by making marginal adjustments to existing rules and procedures. For example, the rules governing the right to vote in presidential primaries could be changed. So-called "open primaries," those which allow adherents of other parties to participate, could be abolished. Such a change, in fact, could perhaps even qualify as a reform, rather than as a retrogression. Allowing Republicans and Independents to vote in the Democratic party's nomination-process comes close to defeating the entire purpose of presidential primaries. When Republicans and Independents constitute nearly 50 percent of an open primary electorate, and when they tend to have candidate preferences different from Democrats, the primary outcome can hardly be called the voice of the party membership. The 1972 Wisconsin primary (where the New Politics faction beat the New Deal faction because of these crossovers) or the 1972 Michigan primary (where the Southern wing topped the other two factions for the same reasons) are cases in point.

By the same token, the rules governing the distribution of delegates from presidential primaries could be manipulated to counteract some of their automatic distortions. Winner-take-all primaries, for example, could be brought back. Such primaries, where the plurality leader acquires the state's entire delegation, would at the very least reduce the number of presidential contenders, and this might reduce the divisiveness of the contest and hence the number of candidate loyalty-induced defections in the general election. In addition, winner-take-all primaries would shift the balance of power within the party away from the medium-sized, homogeneous states and toward large, urban, industrialized states.[2] This would go further in limiting the influence of the Southern and New Politics wings, whose strength is derived from constituents in homogeneous, medium-sized states, and in increasing the influence of the New Deal wing, whose support is found in the urban centers of the large, industrialized states. In addition, winner-take-all rules would also help to negate the unwarranted and disproportionate influence of early delegate selection states (Iowa, New Hampshire) which tend to be sparsely populated and homogeneous, and whose residents tend to be atypical of Democratic party followers.

Finally, the rules could be altered to guarantee less distorted results from presidential primaries, regardless of voter eligibility or delegate allocation. A substantial share of each state's delegation, for example, could be reserved for groups who are underrepresented in primary electorates and for party-related figures, both party officeholders and the party's elected public officials.[3] Reserving seats for underrepresented groups would directly increase the representation and influence of traditional party supporters and the party's general election voters at the national convention. Reserving seats for party-related figures would indirectly compensate for the underrepresentation of traditional party supporters and should, no matter what the ideological leanings of these party figures, inject a more pragmatic perspective into party decisions.

This institutional engineering might be one answer to a basic political and democratic-theoretical dilemma. Such prescriptions would, in short, make the party more likely to be responsive to the types of constituents who also make the party a winner. These prescriptions are, in one sense, an obvious solution, although the politics of implementing them is by no means easy. In fact, in the face of other reforms which tend in the opposite direction, defenders of the party system have often seemed to adopt a purely defensive posture. Instead of taking the initiative and proposing the types of reforms which will return the party to more moderate positions, and to a more competitive stance, they have simply tried to hold the line and, in the process, have ended up gradually relinquishing control to those elements who wish to take the party down a different road. Thus, although cures exist for the terminally ill patient, few are willing to come to its aid. The Southern faction is busy casting wistful eyes toward the Republican party, the New Deal faction is busy praying for a miraculous recovery, and the New Politics faction is busy dividing up what might be a worthless inheritance.

Ironically, a resolution of the Democratic party's dilemma does not necessarily have to come from the rank and file or the leadership of the Democratic party. In fact, much of what the future has in store for that party is heavily conditioned by developments and strategies within the Republican party, perhaps as much or more than by an internal power shift within the Democratic party itself. If the Republican party were to make serious efforts at winning over large chunks of the Southern or even the New Deal wings of the party, the world would look considerably different. In order for this to happen, the Republican party would have to make some changes of its own. It would have to pursue a policy of economic moderation rather than economic conservatism, while it remained aggressively conservative and distinct on foreign policy and social issues. This combined package represents a stiff change, but not an impossible one.

Whether such a change is likely to occur, however, is also, in a perverse fashion, strongly linked to the impact of Democratic party reforms. This is so because those reforms, which were passed by Democratic state legislatures with the national Democratic party in mind, apply to the Republican party as well. The major question is whether Republican party experience in the post-Reform era will parallel Democratic party experience. The proliferation of presidential primaries, on the Republican side, for example, should increase the number of Republican contenders and should raise the competitive level of their contest as well. Evidence since 1972 would seem to support this contention. In both 1972 and 1976 Republican challengers attempted to unseat Republican incumbents who were seeking renomination. In the pre-Reform era, challenges of this nature bordered on treason and were consequently quite rare. In the post-Reform era, on the other hand, they may become commonplace.[4] The absence of a Republican incumbent in 1980 provided the litmus test here. Nine major contenders sought the GOP nomination in 1980, which was nearly twice the average number of Republican contenders during the pre-Reform era.[5]

Competitiveness within the Republican party's nomination process also hurts its electoral prospects, but not to the same degree as it hurts Democrats. Followers of the losing Republican contenders are more likely to defect than followers of the Republican nominee, but they are less likely to defect than followers of losing Democratic contenders. If future Democratic nominations resemble the competitive and sometimes bitter contests of 1972, 1976, and 1980, and if harmonic Republican nominations (Nixon in 1968 and 1972, Reagan in 1980) are more common than bitter and protracted contests (Ford/Reagan in 1976), then the Republicans should receive a much larger net gain in votes, and have a better chance of defeating the battle-damaged Democratic nominee.

In addition, for the Republicans as for the Democrats, presidential primaries also advantage intense, ideological, minorities. In the Republican party, of course, these are conservatives, rather than liberals. What remains true is that primaries (like participatory conventions) reward activists, and today's activists tend to be more ideological than the party membership. But, unlike the activists of the past (party professionals), today's activists (Republican or Democratic) make their candidate and policy decisions with ideology, not general elections, in mind. As a consequence, the Republican nomination process, just as the Democratic nomination process, magnifies the issues and candidate preferences of a minority within the party. And to the extent that that minority is influential, to the same extent the Republican party will probably be uninterested in following the policy strategy that would allow them to pick up disenchanted Democrats.

In the absence of successful attempts to manipulate the rules so as to compensate for many of these problems; in the absence of deliberate tactical moves by the Democratic or Republican leadership to compensate for the same problems; and in the absence of catastrophic events so powerful as to overrule these problems, the future seems reasonably clear. The McGoverns and Reagans will continue to run for their party's nomination and, instead of being discouraged in their efforts, will find that the post-reform rules both encourage and advantage them. Ideologically lopsided pairings, of the Johnson/Goldwater and Nixon/McGovern variety, should become more common. In such cases, predicting presidential elections is easy. Johnson won in 1964, Nixon won in 1972, and the moderate should continue to win in the future. Goldwater lost in 1964, McGovern lost in 1972 and, barring any major crises or postconvention shifts in position, the ideologue should continue to lose. In such scenarios, the only real (and presumably unanswerable) question is who the American people will chose when faced with that inevitable choice between a McGovern and a Goldwater and how the political system will fare under that type of leadership.

In more general terms, it is evident that post-Reform politics will differ significantly from its pre-Reform counterpart. The new rules will usher in an era of principle, not compromise; of ideology, not pragmatism; of conflict, not consensus. It will be an era where personal organizations replace party organizations, and candidate loyalties replace party loyalty. It will be an era of more structural democracy, but less real accountability and practical responsibility. It will be an era of one-term presidents, and hence, an era of weaker presidential leadership and stronger bureaucratic or Congressional leadership. It will be an era of greater governmental expansion and lesser governmental responsiveness, of heightened societal expectations and reduced societal gratifications. It will be an era where all of this will occur because political parties have been gradually reformed into extinction.

NOTES

1. For a further elaboration of this argument, *see* Anthony Downs, *An Economic Theory of Democracy* (New York: Harper and Row, 1957), pp. 96–113.

2. For an assessment of the political effects of various delegate allocation plans, *see* James I. Lengle and Byron Shafer, "Primary Rules, Political Power, and Social Change," *American Political Science Review* 70 (March 1976): 25–40.

3. The Democratic party took a small step in this direction for its 1980 National Convention by reserving a small proportion of each state's delegation for state and local elected officials and by instituting outreach programs for some underrepresented groups (elderly, ethnics, less educated). See Report of the Commission on Presidential Nomination and Party Structure, *Openness, Participation, and Party Building: Reforms for a Stronger Democratic Party* (Washington, D.C.: Democratic National Committee, 1978).

4. Senator Edward Kennedy's challenge of President Jimmy Carter for the 1980 Democratic nomination illustrates this post-Reform era trend in the Democratic party.

5. The nine major contenders for the Republican nomination in 1980 were John Anderson, Howard Baker, George Bush, John Connally, Philip Crane, Robert Dole, Larry Pressler, Ronald Reagan, and Lowell Weicker. Weicker and Pressler dropped out of the contest before the first primary. A tenth candidate, Benjamin Fernandez, contested the nomination from the first primary to the last but failed to receive any serious attention.

APPENDICES

Appendix 1
**Demographic Representation: Party
Registration as a Measure of Party
Membership (California Democratic
Presidential Primary—1972)**

EDUCATION	
8th grade and under	−10
9th–11th grade	−18
High school	−14
1–3 college/bus/tech	0
College degree	+20
Advanced college degree	+33
INCOME	
Under $3,000	−10
$3,000–$6,999	−6
$7,000–$9,999	−6
$10,000–$14,999	+7
$15,000–$19,999	+8
Over $20,000	+9
SOCIAL CLASS	
Lower class	−25
Lower middle class	−11
Middle class	+4
Upper middle/upper class	+13
OCCUPATION	
Laborer/service	−12
Operative/semiskilled	−14
Craftsmen/skilled/foremen	−16
Clerical/sales	+13
Prof/officials/mgrs	0
RACE	
White	+5
Black	−17
Asian/Spanish	−19

SOURCE: California Poll 7204, Field Research
Corporation, San Francisco, Calif.

Appendix 2
Official Primary Results and Yankelovich/*New York Times*/*Time* Survey Results

	FLORIDA		WISCONSIN		PENNSYLVANIA		WISCONSIN	
	Official	*Survey*	*Official*	*Survey*	*Official*	*Survey*	*Official*	*Survey*
Humphrey	19%	18%	21%	22%	35%	33%	16%	16%
McGovern	6%	6%	30%	31%	20%	21%	27%	27%
Wallace	42%	41%	22%	21%	21%	22%	51%	51%
Muskie	9%	9%	10%	11%	20%	21%	2%	2%
Jackson	14%	14%	8%	8%	3%	3%	—	—
Lindsay	7%	7%	7%	7%	—	—	—	—
Chisholm	4%	4%	1%	—	—	—	3%	3%
Other	—	1%	1%	—	—	—	1%	1%
	101%[a]	100%	100%	100%	99%[a]	100%	100%	100%

SOURCE: Recomputed from 1972 *New York Times*/*Time*/Yankelovich, Skelly, and White, Inc. Primary Surveys

[a] Due to rounding

Appendix 3
Demographic Variables: Yankelovich/*New York Times*/*Time* Surveys

	FLORIDA	WISCONSIN	PENNSYLVANIA	MICHIGAN
Age	X	X	X	X
Education	X	:	:	:
Religion	X	X	X	X
Length of residence in state	X	:	:	:
Number of children	X	:	:	:
Sex	X	X	X	X
Occupation of respondent	:	X	X	X
Occupation of chief wage earner	:	X	X	X
Ethnic background	:	X	X	X
Children under 14 years old	:	:	:	X
Income	:	:	:	X
Race	X	X	X	X

SOURCE: Recomputed from 1972 *New York Times*/*Time*/Yankelovich, Skelly, and White, Inc. Primary Surveys

BIBLIOGRAPHY

Alford, Robert R. "Class Voting in Anglo-American Political Systems." In *Party Systems and Voter Alignments: Cross National Perspectives,* edited by Seymour Lipset and Stein Rokkan, pp. 67–94. New York: Free Press, 1967.

Allardt, Erik, and Pesonen, Pertti. "Cleavages in Finnish Politics." In *Party Systems and Voter Alignments: Cross National Perspectives,* edited by Seymour Lipset and Stein Rokkan, pp. 325–66. New York: Free Press, 1967.

Barber, James David, ed. *Choosing the President.* Englewood Cliffs, N.J.: Prentice-Hall, 1974.

Beniger, James R. "Winning the Presidential Nomination: National Polls and State Primary Elections, 1936–1972." *Public Opinion Quarterly* 40 (Spring 1976): 22–38.

Berdahl, Clarence A. "Presidential Selection and Democratic Government." *Journal of Politics* 11 (February 1949): 14–41.

Bernstein, Robert. "Divisive Primaries do Hurt: U.S. Senate Races 1956–1972." *American Political Science Review* 71 (June 1977): 540–45.

Burnham, Walter Dean. *Critical Elections and the Mainsprings of American Politics.* New York: W. W. Norton, 1970.

Butler, David E., and Stokes, Donald. *Political Change in Britain.* New York: St. Martin's Press, 1969.

Campbell, Angus; Converse, Philip E.; Miller, Warren; and Stokes, Donald. *The American Voter.* New York: John Wiley and Sons, 1964.

Carleton, William G. "The Revolution in the Presidential Nominating Convention." *Political Science Quarterly* 72 (June 1957): 224–40.

Cavala, William. "Changing the Rules Changes the Game: Party Reform and the 1972 California Delegation to the Democratic National Convention." *American Political Science Review* 68 (March 1974): 27–42.

Commission on Party Structure and Delegate Selection. *Mandate for Reform.* Washington, D.C.: Democratic National Committee, 1970.

Commission on Presidential Nomination and Party Structure. *Openness, Participation, and Party Building: Reforms for a Stronger Democratic Party.* Washington, D.C.: Democratic National Committee, 1979.

Converse, Philip E. "The Nature of Belief Systems in Mass Publics." In *Ideology and Discontent,* edited by David E. Apter, pp. 238–45. New York: Free Press, 1964.

Converse, Philip E.; Miller, Warren E.; Rusk, Jerrold G.; and Wolfe, Arthur C.

"Continuity and Change in American Politics: Parties and Issues in the 1968 Election." *American Political Science Review* 63 (December 1969): 1083–105.

Dahl, Robert A. *A Preface to Democratic Theory.* Chicago: University of Chicago Press, 1956.

_____, ed. *Political Oppositions in Western Democracies.* New Haven, Conn.: Yale University Press, 1966.

David, Paul T.; Moos, Malcolm; and Goldman, Ralph M. *Presidential Nominating Politics in 1952.* 5 vols. Baltimore: Johns Hopkins Press, 1954.

Davis, James. *Presidential Primaries: Road to the White House.* New York: Thomas Y. Crowell Co., 1967.

Davis, Lanny J. *The Emerging Democratic Majority.* New York: Stein and Day, 1974.

Delegates and Organization Committee. *Programming for the Future, Part 1.* Washington, D.C.: Republican National Committee, 1971.

_____. *The Delegate Selection Procedures for the Republican Party, Part 2.* Washington, D.C.: Republican National Committee, 1971.

Denhart, Robert B., and Hokes, Jay E. "Delegate Selection in Non-Primary States." *National Civic Review* 63 (November 1974): 521–25.

DeVries, Walter, and Tarrance, Lance. *The Ticket Splitters: A New Force in American Politics.* Grand Rapids: Eerdmans, 1972.

DiPalma, Guiseppe, ed. *Mass Politics in Industrial Societies.* Chicago: Markham, 1972.

Downs, Anthony. *An Economic Theory of Democracy.* New York: Harper and Row, 1957.

Epstein, Leon D. *Political Parties in Western Democracies.* New York: Frederick A. Praeger, 1967.

Ernst, Harry W. *The Primary That Made a President: West Virginia, 1960.* New York: McGraw-Hill, 1962.

Greenstein, Fred I. *The American Party System and the American People.* Englewood Cliffs, N.J.: Prentice-Hall, 1970.

Hacker, Andrew. "Does a 'Divisive' Primary Harm a Candidate's Election Chances." *American Political Science Review* 59 (March 1965): 105–10.

Hadley, Arthur T. *The Invisible Primary.* Englewood Cliffs, N.J.: Prentice-Hall, 1976.

Jennings, M. Kent, and Niemi, Richard G. *The Political Character of Adolescence: The Influence of Families and Schools.* Princeton: Princeton University Press, 1974.

Jewell, Malcolm E. "A Caveat on the Expanding Use of Presidential Primaries." *Policy Studies Journal* (Summer 1974): 279–84.

Johnson, Donald, and Gibson, James. "The Divisive Primary Revisited: Party Activists in Iowa." *American Political Science Review* 68 (March 1974): 67–77.

Keech, William R. "Anticipating the Consequences of a National Presidential Primary." *Policy Studies Journal* (Summer 1974): 274–79.

Keech, William R., and Matthews, Donald R. *The Party's Choice.* Washington, D.C.: Brookings Institution, 1976.

Key, V. O. *American State Politics*. New York: Alfred A. Knopf, 1956.
————. *Public Opinion and American Democracy*. New York: Alfred A. Knopf, 1960.
————. *Politics, Parties, and Pressure Groups*. New York: Thomas Y. Crowell Co., 1964.
————. *The Responsible Electorate*. Cambridge: Harvard University Press, 1966.
Kirkpatrick, Jeane J. "Representation in American National Conventions: The Case of 1972." *British Journal of Political Science* 5 (1975): 265–322.
Kravits, Walter. *Presidential Preference Primaries, 1928–1956*. Washington, D.C.: Library of Congress, 1960.
Lazarsfeld, Paul; Berelson, Bernard; and Gaudet, Hazel. *The People's Choice*. New York: Columbia University Press, 1948.
Lee, Eugene, and Keith, Bruce. *California Votes, 1960–1972*. Berkeley: Institute of Governmental Studies, 1974.
Lengle, James I., and Shafer, Byron. "Primary Rules, Political Power, and Social Change." *American Political Science Review* 70 (March 1976): 27–42.
Linz, Juan J. "Cleavage and Consensus in West German Politics." In *Party Systems and Voter Alignments: Cross National Perspectives*, edited by Seymour Lipset and Stein Rokkan, pp. 283–324. New York: Free Press, 1967.
Lipset, Seymour, and Rokkan, Stein, eds. *Party Systems and Voter Alignments: Cross National Perspectives*. New York: Free Press, 1967.
Lucy, William H. "Polls, Primaries, and Presidential Nominations." *Journal of Politics* 35 (November 1973): 830–48.
Marshall, Thomas R. "Delegate Selection in Non-Primary States: The Question of Representation." *National Civic Review* (September 1976): 390–93.
Matthews, Donald R., ed. *Perspectives on Presidential Selection*. Washington, D.C.: Brookings Institution, 1973.
McClosky, Herbert; Hoffmann, Paul J.; and O'Hara, Rosemary. "Issue Conflict and Consensus among Party Leaders and Followers." *American Political Science Review* 54 (June 1960): 406–27.
Morris, William D., and Davis, Otto. "The Sport of Kings: Turnout in Presidential Preference Primaries." Paper delivered at the American Political Science Association Convention, San Francisco, September, 1975.
Nie, Norman H.; Verba, Sidney; and Petrocik, John R. *The Changing American Voter*. Cambridge: Harvard University Press, 1976.
Niemi, Richard G., and Weisberg, Herbert. *Controversies in American Voting Behavior*. San Francisco: W. H. Freeman, 1976.
Overacker, Louise. *Presidential Primaries*. New York: Macmillan Co., 1926.
Pennock, J. Roland, and Chapman, John W., eds. *Representation: Nomos X*. New York: Atherton Press, 1968.
Phillips, Kevin P. *The Emerging Republican Majority*. New Rochelle, N.Y.: Arlington House, 1969.
Pitkin, Hanna Fenichel. *The Concept of Representation*. Berkeley: University of California Press, 1967.
Polsby, Nelson W. *Political Promises: Essays and Commentary in American Politics*. New York: Oxford University Press, 1974.

Polsby, Nelson W., and Wildavsky, Aaron. *Presidential Elections*. New York: Charles Scribner's Sons, 1976.

Pomper, Gerald M. *Nominating the President*. New York: W. W. Norton, 1966.

————. "From Confusion to Clarity: Issues and American Voters, 1956–1968." *American Political Science Review* 66 (June 1972): 415–28.

Presidential Elections Since 1789. Washington, D.C.: Congressional Quarterly Inc., 1979.

Ranney, Austin, "The Representativeness of Primary Electorates." *Midwest Journal of Political Science* 12 (May 1968): 224–38.

————. "Turnout and Representation in Presidential Primary Elections." *American Political Science Review* 66 (March 1972): 21–37.

————. *Curing the Mischiefs of Factions: Party Reform in America*. Berkeley: University of California Press, 1975.

————. *Participation in American Presidential Nominations, 1976*. Washington, D.C.: American Enterprise Institute, 1977.

Ranney, Austin, and Epstein, Leon. "The Two Electorates: Voters and Nonvoters in a Wisconsin Primary." *Journal of Politics* 28 (August 1966): 598–616.

RePass, David. "Issue Salience and Party Choice." *American Political Science Review* 65 (June 1971): 389–400.

Roper, Burns W. "Distorting the Voice of the People." *Columbia Journalism Review* 14 (November–December 1975): 28–32.

Sorauf, Frank J. *Party Politics in America*. 3d ed. Boston: Little, Brown and Co., 1976.

Statement of Vote: State of California, 1968 Primary Election. Sacramento: Secretary of State's Office, 1968.

Statement of Vote: State of California, 1972 Primary Election. Sacramento: Secretary of State's Office, 1972.

Stokes, Donald E. "Some Dynamic Elements of Contests for the Presidency." *American Political Science Review* 60 (March 1966): 19–28.

Verba, Sidney, and Nie, Norman H. *Participation in America: Political Democracy and Social Equality*. New York: Harper and Row, 1972.

White, Theodore. *The Making of the President 1960*. New York: Atheneum, 1961.

————. *The Making of the President 1964*. New York: Atheneum, 1965.

————. *The Making of the President 1968*. New York: Atheneum, 1969.

————. *The Making of the President 1972*. New York: Atheneum, 1973.

Williams, Daniel C. "Voter Decisionmaking in a Primary Election: An Evaluation of Three Models of Choice." *American Journal of Political Science* 20 (February 1976): 37–49.

Wise, Sidney. "Choosing the Presidential Candidates." *Current History* 67 (August 1974): 52–57.

Wolfinger, Raymond E., and Rosenstone, Steven J. *Who Votes?* New Haven: Yale University Press, 1980.

Zeidenstein, Harvey. "Presidential Primaries—Reflections of the People's Choice?" *Journal of Politics* 32 (November 1970): 856–74.

INDEX

About the Author

James I. Lengle is Assistant Professor of Political Science at Georgetown University, Washington, D.C. His writings have appeared in the *American Political Science Review* and *American Politics Quarterly*. He has also coedited a book on the presidential nomination and election process.